LONGMAN CRITICAL

A MIDSUMMER NIGHT'S DREAM

William Shakespeare

Editors:
Linda Cookson
Bryan Loughrey

Longman Critical Essays

Editors: Linda Cookson and Bryan Loughrey

Titles in the series:

CONTENTS

PREFACE

Like all professional groups, literary critics have developed their own specialised language. This is not necessarily a bad thing. Sometimes complex concepts can only be described in a terminology far removed from everyday speech. Academic jargon, however, creates an unnecessary barrier between the critic and the intelligent but less practised reader.

This danger is particularly acute where scholarly books and articles are re-packaged for a student audience. Critical anthologies, for example, often contain extracts from longer studies originally written for specialists. Deprived of their original context, these passages can puzzle and at times mislead. The essays in this volume, however, are all specially commissioned, self-contained works, written with the needs of students firmly in mind.

This is not to say that the contributors — all experienced critics and teachers — have in any way attempted to simplify the complexity of the issues with which they deal. On the contrary, they explore the central problems of the text from a variety of critical perspectives, reaching conclusions which are challenging and at times mutually contradictory.

They try, however, to present their arguments in a direct, accessible language and to work within the limitations of scope and length which students inevitably face. For this reason, essays are generally rather briefer than is the practice; they address quite specific topics; and, in line with examination requirements, they incorporate precise textual detail into the body of the discussion.

They offer, therefore, working examples of the kind of essay-writing skills which students themselves are expected to develop. Their diversity, however, should act as a reminder that in the field of literary studies there is no such thing as a 'model' answer. Good essays are the outcome of a creative engagement with literature, of sensitive, attentive reading and careful thought. We hope that those contained in this volume will encourage students to return to the most important starting point of all, the text itself, with renewed excitement and the determination to explore more fully their own critical responses.

How to use this volume

Obviously enough, you should start by reading the text in question. The one assumption that all the contributors make is that you are already familiar with this. It would be helpful, of course, to have read further — perhaps other works by the same author or by influential contemporaries. But we don't assume that you have yet had the opportunity to do this and any references to historical background or to other works of literature are explained.

You should, perhaps, have a few things to hand. It is always a good idea to keep a copy of the text nearby when reading critical studies. You will almost certainly want to consult it when checking the context of quotations or pausing to consider the validity of the critic's interpretation. You should also try to have access to a good dictionary, and ideally a copy of a dictionary of literary terms as well. The contributors have tried to avoid jargon and to express themselves clearly and directly. But inevitably there will be occasional words or phrases with which you are unfamiliar. Finally, we would encourage you to make notes, summarising not just the argument of each essay but also your own responses to what you have read. So keep a pencil and notebook at the ready.

Suitably equipped, the best thing to do is simply begin with whichever topic most interests you. We have deliberately organised each volume so that the essays may be read in any order. One consequence of this is that, for the sake of clarity and self-containment, there is occasionally a degree of overlap between essays. But at least you are not forced to follow one — fairly arbitrary — reading sequence.

Each essay is followed by brief 'Afterthoughts', designed to highlight points of critical interest. But remember, these are only there to remind you that it is *your* responsibility to question what you read. The essays printed here are not a series of 'model' answers to be slavishly imitated and in no way should they be regarded as anything other than a guide or stimulus for your own thinking. We hope for a critically involved response: 'That was interesting. But if *I* were tackling the topic . . . !'

Read the essays in this spirit and you'll pick up many of the skills of critical composition in the process. We have, however, tried to provide more explicit advice in 'A practical guide to essay writing'. You may find this helpful, but do not imagine it offers any magic formulas. The quality of your essays ultimately depends on the quality of your engagement with literary texts. We hope this volume spurs you on to read these with greater understanding and to explore your responses in greater depth.

A note on the text

All references are to the New Penguin Shakespeare edition of *A Midsummer Night's Dream*, ed. Stanley Wells.

Kate Flint

Kate Flint is Fellow and Tutor in English Literature at Mansfield College, Oxford. She is the author of numerous critical works.

ESSAY

A Midsummer Night's Dream: the power of transformation

A Midsummer Night's Dream is about transformations. In it, Shakespeare explores questions concerning the relationship between theatre and the real world, of how art can be turned into life and vice versa. The main source for his subject-matter was Ovid's *Metamorphoses*, the prime classical collection of myths of transformation. More specifically, he emphasises this theme by presenting a play within a play. But the essential faculty which allows such transformations to take place is imagination, and Shakepeare's fascination with this faculty lies at the heart of the play.

A casual glance at the world of the fairy rulers, Titania and Oberon, served by a mischievous Puck and a host of lesser sprites, has misled many producers and designers into showing them inhabiting a lyrically pretty environment. And the 'rude mechanicals', rehearsing their production of *Pyramus and Thisbe* are still, too frequently, regarded merely as comics, presenting a heavy-handed parody of a dramatic performance; members of a working class who, in their hopelessly inept efforts at amateur dramatics, need not be treated seriously. But *A Midsummer Night's Dream* is a much more disturbing play than, on the surface, one might be tempted to assume. Much of the action takes place at night, in a world ruled by the moon: a world, therefore, of changeability, where rational daylight no longer provides illumination; a world of dreams, where the unconscious and its energies are released.

While the formal structure of the play celebrates a marriage, its language often suggests that sexuality is not something which is necessarily easily controllable by social bondings. The images used to describe love and desire are, at the start, conventional enough. Theseus speaks of winning one's love by the sword (although even then, one might think of this as a conspicuously phallic, as well as war-like term, when employed for a victory over the Queen of the fiercest of women, the Amazons). In Hermia and Lysander's dialogue there are images of roses and rain which seem to have been plucked from Elizabethan lyric poetry: 'How now, my love? Why is your cheek so pale?', Lysander asks his beloved: 'How chance the roses there do fade so fast?' 'Belike for want of rain,' Hermia replies, 'which I could well/ Beteem them from the tempest of my eyes' (I.1.128–131). And she goes on to proclaim her allegiance to Lysander in a set of conventional emblems:

> I swear to thee by Cupid's strongest bow,
> By his best arrow with the golden head,
> By the simplicity of Venus' doves,
> By that which knitteth souls and prospers loves

> (I.1.169–172)

But how reliable a being is Cupid? In Helena's soliloquy which ends the first scene, she points to the part that the winged messenger of the god of love can play in the whole business of transformation:

> Things base and vile, holding no quantity,
> Love can transpose to form and dignity.
> Love looks not with the eyes, but with the mind,
> And therefore is winged Cupid painted blind.

> (I.1.232–235)

Here, Helena is using a Renaissance commonplace: the idea, as the Renaissance Italian philosopher Pico della Mirandola put it, that Love is blind 'because he is above the intellect'. Love, she is suggesting, falls out of line with rationality: instead, it is linked to the powers of imagination and the creation of poetry. Helena hints that someone in its power sees only what he or she *wants* to see and thus, one might say, it releases the desires of the unconscious. But rather than this awakening of the unconscious being some elevating, mystical process, it may, in fact, bring one into line with forces which represent quite the reverse. For the blind Eros, in the Renaissance, was also known as a wanton god, a demon who would befuddle the intelligence of humans through arousing their animal appetites. Blind pleasure, unguided by reason, was deceptive, corrupting, short-lived. The Renaissance problem posed by the figure of blind Cupid centred around the differing interpretations of the word *voluptas* (the Latin word for sexual desire) — used of the most primitive and the most exalted forms of pleasure. Among other things, *A Midsummer Night's Dream* deals not just with the transformations which love, or *voluptas*, can cause, but also shows us how understanding of the word 'love' itself may be transformed.

In Helena's speech, Cupid seems a figure of manic desire: 'Wings and no eyes figure uneasy haste' (I.1.237). Such desire is bestial, rather than human. Helena herself, in Act II scene 1, shows her collapse from self-respect into a willingness to become a masochistic lap-dog:

> I am your spaniel; and, Demetrius,
> The more you beat me I will fawn on you.
> Use me but as your spaniel: spurn me, strike me
>
> (II.1.203–205)

Later, self-deprecating, she protests 'I am as ugly as a bear' (II.2.100), and Hermia also descends to the insults of the animal world when roused against Helena: 'She was a vixen when she went to school' (III.2.324). By using such imagery, the women are drawing themselves into the animal sphere of the fairy wood: it is not an Arcadia, but rather a repository of all the evil creatures a witch or sorcerer might use. Spotted snakes, thorny hedgehogs, newts, blindworms, long-legged poisonous spiders, black-beetles, worms and snails belong, in their odiousness, alongside the toad, fenny snake, frog, bat, adder, lizard and owlet of *Macbeth*'s witches' brew. The live ingredients which crop up in the *Dream* are not arbitrary nasty creatures, but could be found in medieval and Renaissance prescriptions for curing both impotence and various women's disorders. Moreover, in their stickiness, creepiness, and repulsiveness to the touch, they create aversions which have subsequently figured prominently in psychoanalytic studies of sexual neurosis. They form typical elements in the bestiary of Freud's theory of dreams — lizards, for example, he relates to the fear of castration, since they are creatures whose tails grow again if pulled off, and snakes are 'those most important symbols of the male organ': both observations are taken from a section in *The Interpretation of Dreams* where he maintains that 'Many of the beasts which are used as genital symbols in mythology and folklore play the same part in dreams.' Thus oberon's order to Puck, to lead the lovers 'Till o'er their brows death-counterfeiting sleep/ With leaden legs and batty wings doth creep' (III.2.364–365) seems, apart from anything else, an encouragement for them to be brought into contact with their own motivating sexual desires. Puck himself, of course, is far more sinister than the mischievous hobgoblin he is sometimes presented as being. At the time when the play was written, Puck had long been one of the recognised names for the devil. He is deceptive: on the one hand the relatively benevolent household spirit, Robin Goodfellow, yet on the other having the power to change and multiply his shape into a variety of animal forms:

> Sometimes a horse I'll be, sometime a hound,
> A hog, a headless bear, sometime a fire,
> And neigh, and bark, and grunt and roar and burn
> Like horse, hound, hog, bear, fire at every turn.
>
> (III.1.103–106

What, then, in relation to all this, is to be made of Oberon's wishing Bottom onto Titania, exercising his own masculine authority over her, just as Egeus attempts to dominate Hermia's marital decision in the world of the court? Oberon wishes to punish Titania for withholding from him the Indian boy that he wants as his own follower. Even in this conflict, there are disruptive sexual overtones. While Oberon clearly has heterosexual tastes — has he not had a fling with his 'warrior love'

Hippolyta before the play begins? — his desire for the young boy, like his very promiscuity, is mildly disruptive. Titania's punishment, as Oberon sees it, is to take an animal as her lover:

> The next thing then she, waking, looks upon —
> Be it on lion, bear, or wolf, or bull,
> On meddling monkey or on busy ape —
> She shall pursue it with the soul of love.
>
> (II.1.179–182)

The selection of animals is a deliberate one:

> Be it ounce or cat or bear,
> Pard, or boar with bristled hair
>
> (II.2.36–37)

since all of these are creatures which, in Shakespeare's time, were considered to represent sexual potency. Bottom's transformation into an ass, too, would not so much have allowed the original audience to laugh at his docile stupidity but to wonder at his sexuality, since from antiquity up to the Renaissance, asses were credited with amazing potency, and among all quadrupeds were supposed to have the longest and hardest phallus. But remember:

> Things base and vile, holding no quantity,
> Love can transpose to form and dignity.
>
> (I.1.232–233)

Titania hardly objects, therefore, in her midsummer dream state, to this rapturously repulsive union with an ass. The magical, dream-like circumstances allow the release of her own animal desires which, nonetheless, are still expressed through the lyrical language associated with more orthodox patterns of courtship:

> Come, sit thee down upon this flowery bed
> While I thy amiable cheeks do coy,
> And stick muskroses in thy sleek, smooth head,
> And kiss thy fair large ears, my gentle joy.
>
> (IV.1.1–4)

However, erotic fantasy can only be liberated, without shame, in an unreal, midsummer's moonlit night: a world where partners can be freely exchanged, unlike the real world, where they have to be carefully matched with regard to status and income. In the wood, partners are chosen because they are to hand, not because they are who they are. Names and faces cease to matter. Titania is horrified when daylight comes:

> TITANIA My Oberon, what visions have I seen!
> Methought I was enamoured of an ass.
> OBERON There lies your love.
> TITANIA   How came these things to pass?
> O, how mine eyes do loathe his visage now!
>
> (IV.1.75–78)

Bottom, on the other hand, is left not horrified, but speechless, having had access, in a world of dream, to an experience outside the wildest conscious imaginings of an Athenian weaver. Afraid to bring into being, through language, what he has lived through, he censors his experience, as though thrusting it back into the realm of the unconscious:

> Methought I was — there is no man can tell what. Methought I was — and methought I had — but man is but a patched fool if he will offer to say what methought I had.
>
> (IV.1.205–208)

The young lovers, unsurprisingly, emerge from this midnight romp with the correct partners, their initial preference counting for nothing. Their experience has been akin to the magic of a fairy-tale, a genre which traditionally makes much use of magical woods. Bruno Bettelheim, in *The Uses of Enchantment* (1976), usefully summarises their special properties:

> In many European fairy tales the brother who leaves soon finds himself in a deep, dark forest, where he feels lost, having given up the organisation of his life which the parental home provided, and not yet having built up the inner structures which we develop only under the impact of life experiences which we have to master more or less on our own. Since ancient times the near-impenetrable forest in which we get lost has symbolised the dark, hidden, near-impenetrable world of our unconscious. If we have lost the framework which gave structure to our past life and must now find our way to become ourselves, and have entered this wilderness with an as yet undeveloped personality,

when we succeed in finding our way out we shall emerge with a much more highly developed humanity.

In this case, the humanity which has been achieved is not so much a development of personality, of individuality, but an achievement of a more human, less animal type of love, a metamorphosis of the physical towards the spiritual and thus more god-like. Theseus, out hunting, greets the young lovers:

> Good morrow, friends — Saint Valentine is past!
> Begin these woodbirds but to couple now?
>
> (IV.1.138–139)

Woodbirds, doves — holy spirits is perhaps pushing the point too far, but nonetheless a higher point on the chain of being, a higher form of *voluptas*, seems to have been achieved.

It has been achieved, however, with little effort or prolonged suffering. Well might Demetrius ask:

> Are you sure
> That we are awake? It seems to me
> That yet we sleep, we dream.
>
> (IV.1.191–193)

He retains sufficient grasp on probability to realise that such neat patternings can exist only in a world of dream-desire — or, for that matter, in the artifices of poetry and drama. And it is important to think further about creative imagination, and about the power of drama itself, in considering the sub-plot of the play. *A Midsummer Night's Dream*, as I've discussed it so far, could well come to a conclusion with the happy nuptials promised at the very beginning of Act V. But the performance of Bottom and his crew serves ends beyond those of allowing Titania an opportunity to act out some sexual fantasies with an animal — or with a working-class man, a more pertinent form of transgression — earlier in the play.

Pyramus and Thisbe presents alternative means of examining some of the themes encountered in the main action. The events in the Athenian forest have, through art and magic, ended with the happy unions characteristic of the conclusion to a comedy, but in the mechanicals' production we have a reminder, albeit distanced through fatuous language, of how division and discord can end in tragedy. The lovers, divided by a wall erected by their fathers, cannot touch each other, can only see each other through a crack: an emblematic way of reworking the difficulties faced by Hermia in her questioning of her father's authority. In *Pyramus and Thisbe*, wild animals are not conveniently banished to the medium of suggestive language, but, like barriers between lovers, are made visible: a hungry lion comes roaring to the rendezvous and frightens off Thisbe, who drops her mantle. Pyramus discovers the blood-stained rag, attacks nature for her cruelty — 'Since lion vile hath here deflowered my dear' (V.1.284) (a malapropism which reminds us of the potential closeness of human and animal sexual relations) — and commits suicide. Thisbe, returning, finds his bloody corpse, and stabs herself to death:

> Tongue, not a word!
> Come, trusty sword,
> Come blade, my breast imbrue!
> And farewell friends.
> Thus Thisbe ends.
> Adieu, adieu, adieu!

> (V.1.334–339)

However ridiculous this may intentionally sound, it's worth bearing in mind that the plot of *Pyramus and Thisbe* is almost identical to that of *Romeo and Juliet*, written around the same time. What takes place on stage on this occasion is yet another form of transformation: tragedy into comedy.

Bottom, Quince, Snug, Flute and the rest are workmen — a carpenter, a joiner, a weaver, a bellows-mender, a tinker and a tailor. They come from a class seldom seen in such detail in Shakespeare's theatre, and, at one level, are not treated particularly fairly: their efforts are presented as comic, and the Athenian audience make sophisticated fun at their expense, perpetually interrupting and mocking their performance. The company is shown — again not particularly seriously — as being concerned about how their show will be received before exalted company. 'Let me play the lion too,' says Bottom, anxious, as always, to prove himself the best man for any possible part:

> BOTTOM I will roar that will do any man's heart good to hear me. I will roar that I will make the Duke say 'Let him roar again; let him roar again!'

QUINCE   An you should do it too terribly you would fright the
         Duchess and the ladies that they would shriek; and that
         were enough to hang us all.
ALL   That would hang us, every mother's son.

(I.2.66–73)

How should this problem be resolved? The answer, for these
workmen, is clear. The audience must be made aware that they
are watching a play, not a real rapacious feline:

SNOUT   Therefore another prologue must tell he is not a lion.
BOTTOM   Nay, you must name his name, and half his face must
         be seen through the lion's neck, and he himself must speak
         through, saying thus, or to the same defect: 'Ladies', or 'Fair
         ladies — I would wish you', or 'I would request you', or 'I
         would entreat you — not to fear, not to tremble. My life for
         yours: if you think I come hither as a lion, it were pity of my
         life. No. I am no such thing. I am a man, as other men are'
         — and there indeed let him name his name, and tell them
         plainly he is Snug the joiner.

(III.1.31–42)

Shakespeare is here taking up one of his favourite themes:
the relationship between art and life. But rather than indicating,
as Hamlet does when speaking to the Players, that art, that
acting, should 'hold, as 'twere, the mirror up to nature' (*Hamlet*,
III.2.21–2), here the very upside-down nature of having the
working-class characters speak about such an important matter
leads to the reversal of such a proposition: even within the
theatre, one should be aware that what one is watching is not
real, but make-believe. Only, of course, one is caught in a double
bind. For in order to believe in the statement, one is asked to
believe in the reality of Bottom the weaver; that he is an actual
Athenian working man: 'a man, as other men are'. As other men
are — as Theseus, as Lysander, as Egeus — free from the class-
based distinctions which order Athenian — or for that matter
Elizabethan — society.

By this, I do not want to suggest crudely that Shakespeare
is making a radical political statement. We are encouraged too
frequently to laugh at the efforts of the rough players for this to
be the case. But the introduction of the play within the play into
the final act, the return to apparent normality after the

excursion into the fairy world, does suggest a Chinese box effect: the existence of different layers on which the real and the imaginary, the conscious and the unconscious interact. This impression is strengthened by the very end of the play. It is no earthly figure of authority, such as Theseus, who begs for the audience's applause at the end, but the manipulator of the love-plot, Puck, with a little lyrical help from Oberon and Titania. 'If we shadows have offended,' Puck tells the audience:

> Think but this, and all is mended:
> That you have but slumbered here
> While these visions did appear.
> And this weak and idle theme,
> No more yielding but a dream,
> Gentles, do not reprehend.

(V.1.413–419)

Drama, dream, shadows, the fairy world, the unconscious: Shakespeare's play, despite the happy note of unity on which it ends, does not offer any neat conclusions about the interaction of these themes. It is indeed a drama of transformations, where, under special circumstances, all sorts of desires, social, political, and sexual, can temporarily take material form. Indeed, as *A Midsummer Night's Dream* suggests, the theatre may provide a special, contained place in which such desires may safely be acted out, before 'normal' order is restored. Nevertheless, it is in the nature of desire, and, more broadly, of the unconscious, that they retain their disruptive power, defying the attempts of rational humanity to contain them. The plot of the play may suggest that unsettling transformations are righted in terms of social relations, but the play's language ensures that no such easy resolution of the powerful forces exerted by desire and the imagination can be possible in our own minds.

AFTERTHOUGHTS

What 'transformations' does Flint explore in this essay?

What links are suggested in this essay between human and animal worlds?

What thematic importance does Flint attach to the performance of *Pyramus and Thisbe*?

Has this essay convinced you of Flint's initial contention that 'A *Midsummer Night's Dream* is a much more disturbing play than, on the surface, one might be tempted to assume' (page 10)?

T O Treadwell

*T O Treadwell lectures in English at
Roehampton Institute, and is the author
of numerous critical studies.*

ESSAY

A Midsummer Night's Dream and the nature of comedy

One very plausible theory for the origin of drama locates its roots in the ritual life of the earliest human civilisations. As men and women developed a sense of their dependence on the earth and the other creatures they shared it with, so this theory goes, they began to devise rituals to express their understanding of the natural world around them and to try to influence it on their behalf. As civilisation developed, the original meaning of these early rituals became disguised or distorted but the rituals themselves endured because they continued to express something enduring about the forces that shape human life — the mysteries of birth, death, and sexuality, the movement from day to night and from summer to winter. Gradually, the ceremonies devised to explain or celebrate these forces developed into drama, but they retained something of their ritual quality, and because the matters they originally dealt with are so fundamental, they continue to exercise imaginative power.

One of the most basic of these ancient ritual patterns is that having to do with fertility, with death and rebirth, both in nature and in human life. Rituals of this kind imitate all those patterns in our lives in which an initial defeat becomes a final victory — winter turns to spring, war ends in peace, death is followed by rebirth. This pattern assumes that something has to 'die' in order for something better to come into being, but because the pattern ends 'happily' with the birth of something better rituals of this sort, when they evolve into drama, take the form of comedy.

The basic death and rebirth plot, both in ritual and drama, takes the form of a conflict between a hero or heroine, called the *protagonist* and an *antagonist* who tries to block the progress represented by the protagonist (*agon* is the Greek word for 'conflict'). Thus the protagonist can be a figure like Life, Spring, the New Year, the New King, the New God, or the Son, while the opposing antagonist will be Death, Winter, the Old Year, the Old King, the Old God, or the Father. Often, the protagonist appears to be weaker or less effective than he actually is and the antagonist appears to be stronger or more powerful than he actually is. We can see this ancient pattern at work very clearly in the countless stories we have in which an apparently weak or inadequate hero overcomes a seemingly all-powerful opponent — stories like those of David and Goliath or Jack and the Giant.

In the earliest Greek comedies a set of stock characters developed to fulfil the functions of this basic plot. The protagonist was called the *eiron*, a word which is usually translated as 'self-deprecator' (our word 'irony' is derived from it) and which refers to the protagonist's characteristic quality of seeming to be less effective or less intelligent than is actually the case. The antagonist was called the *alazon*, which means 'impostor' and which stresses that this character only *seems* to be all-powerful and frightening. A third stock character was the *bomolochos* or buffoon, whose antics added an extra comic dimension to the plot; because he often pretends to be stupider or more ignorant than he really is, the *bomolochos* sometimes merges with the character of the *eiron*, but often appears separately.

From the *eiron* develops the hero or heroine of comedy, the character we find attractive, the one we hope to see succeed, the one who gets the girl or the boy in the end. The *eiron* is often accompanied by (or identified with) the *bomolochos*, the witty servant, the clown, jester, or trickster, crafty and unscrupulous, on whom so many of the world's comedies depend for the resolution of their plots. Deriving from the *alazon* are all those figures who threaten, bluster or block: boastful giants and bullies, despots and tyrants, miserly fathers and wicked stepmothers. These characters seem at first to be too powerful for the *eiron* and there is usually a stage in which the hero or heroine is somehow defeated by them, but this defeat turns out to be only temporary and the *alazon* is ultimately overcome — thus reflecting, in comic form, the ancient ritual pattern of death and rebirth.

A second standard pattern for comedy, also deriving from primitive ritual, is the motif of the feast or festival where normal social distinctions and rules of behaviour are overturned or ignored so that, however briefly, the participants can experience freedom from the conventions that normally rule their lives. Feasts of this sort have been common all over the world and are documented from the earliest times of which we have record; among many examples are the Greek Dionysia, the Roman Saturnalia, the medieval Feast of Fools, and the carnival before Lent which is still an important event in many cultures in our own day. These feasts were (and are) often riotous and debauched. They almost always contained an element of mockery aimed at the most solemn and important social and religious institutions, nothing being too sacred to be parodied or ridiculed. In the great houses of Elizabethan England, for example, the elaborate feasts held to celebrate Christmas commonly included the election of a 'Lord of Misrule', often a lowly member of the household, who, for a brief period, was licensed to take the place of the actual lord and to preside over a Bacchanalian evening during which all the usual forms of subordination and propriety were overthrown. Elizabethan society, like most other societies, was stratified and formal, and the feast presided over by the Lord of Misrule offered a momentary release from the restraints of propriety and formality which the demands of social order were thought to make necessary.

In comic drama, the motif of the feast is reflected in the creation of a world where everything is topsy-turvy, where none of the ordinary rules of life apply, where roles are reversed, identities are mistaken or lost, and the ruling spirit is mystery and confusion. Just as in the real world the feast comes to an end, former identities are resumed, and the old social order is re-established, so in the world of the play all this comic anarchy is finally sorted out and the characters returned to a sense of normality, but very often it is the experience of the chaos and confusion that allows the happy ending to take place.

With the partial exception of his very early play *The Comedy of Errors*, all Shakespeare's comedies exhibit the same structural pattern, a basic plot which has been central to comedy since the time of the ancient Roman playwrights Plautus and Terence and which continues to appear in various forms today. Comedy based on this pattern is usually called 'romantic comedy'; it is one of the most popular and enduring of literary forms, and can clearly be seen to develop out of the broader structural patterns we have been discussing. In this basic plot, a young man and a young woman desire each other, but find that various forces prevent them from fulfilling this desire. The main action of the comedy consists in the overcoming of these forces, and at the end of the play the young lovers are triumphantly brought together in marriage.

Because the protagonists in romantic comedy are almost always *young* lovers, the antagonists standing in the way of the successful fulfilment of their love are usually *old* people, most commonly parents; the happy ending of this sort of comedy therefore normally involves the defeat of the old by the young. At the beginning of the story, the young lovers find themselves in a society where the older generation has the power to deny them their wishes, so that the final victory over the older generation usually involves a victory over the society that the old people control — a world that was crabbed, harsh and repressive becomes one that is loving, giving and free.

Of the various forces that societies use to exercise control over their members, one of the most important is the *law*, and the brilliant critic Northrop Frye has pointed out how often Shakespeare's comedies contain a harsh or irrational law as the blocking force standing between the young lovers and their desires. At the beginning of *A Midsummer Night's Dream*, for example, the *eiron* Hermia wishes to marry Lysander, but her desire is thwarted by her father Egeus, a typical blustering *alazon*, who intends her to marry Demetrius even though this

young man is no more 'worthy' than Lysander. The opening
scene is set in Athens, and it is made clear that Athens is a
repressive society which supports the rights of parents to impose
their will on their children. Egeus's first substantial speech
makes this entirely explicit:

> I beg the ancient privilege of Athens:
> As she is mine, I may dispose of her;
> Which shall be either to this gentleman
> Or to her death, according to our law
> Immediately provided in that case.
>
> (I.1.41–45)

Nothing could be clearer. Hermia belongs to her father —
he can 'dispose' of her however he pleases, and the society of
Athens provides a law in support of his right to do so. At the
head of Athenian society is Theseus, the Duke, who is disposed
to be sympathetic to lovers — he is one himself, after all — but
whose primary responsibility as a ruler is to uphold the law.
Hermia must subject herself to it:

> For you, fair Hermia, look you arm yourself
> To fit your fancies to your father's will;
> Or else the law of Athens yields you up —
> Which by no means we may extenuate —
> To death or to a vow of single life.
>
> (I.1.117–121)

Theseus is speaking as a responsible ruler here; his duty is to
uphold the law and he must never 'extenuate' or undermine it.

The law to which Egeus appeals is interestingly specific.
When Hermia asks the Duke what her punishment will be
should she refuse to wed Demetrius, Theseus replies:

> Either to die the death, or to abjure
> For ever the society of men.
> Therefore, fair Hermia, question your desires,
> Know of your youth, examine well your blood,
> Whether, if you yield not to your father's choice,
> You can endure the livery of a nun,
> For aye to be in shady cloister mewed,

To live a barren sister all your life,
Chanting faint hymns to the cold fruitless moon.

(I.1.65–73)

What this law really attacks is Hermia's *fertility*. Unless she submits to her father's right to control her marriage-choice she must either be executed (this option is very lightly stressed) or retire to a nunnery where, of course, strict chastity is enforced. Theseus's language is full of images of infertility: Hermia is to be pent up in a 'shady cloister' shut away from the sun's ripening rays; she must be permanently 'barren', devoting herself to worshipping a moon specifically called 'cold' and 'fruitless'. *A Midsummer Night's Dream* is set in pagan Greece, so the moon goddess whom Hermia will be condemned to worship is Artemis or Diana, who is also the goddess associated with chastity. Hermia's hymns to the moon will be 'faint', and this detail associates chastity with weakness, sickliness, and lack of energy. If we remember the theory that locates the origin of the most fundamental comic structures in ancient fertility rituals, we will see the appropriateness of this. The force that Hermia must overcome is the law that threatens her freedom to express her sexuality as she wishes, that will condemn her to a sterile existence and deny her the right to fulfil her proper destiny, which is to marry and thus to take her part in the creation of new life. *A Midsummer Night's Dream*, then, begins with the heroine threatened by an *alazon* figure clearly identified with age, sterility and death whose tyrannical behaviour is fully supported by society and its laws.

By the end of the play, all this has changed. Egeus does not appear again until Act IV scene 1, when he enters the woods with Theseus and Hippolyta and discovers the four young lovers, now sorted out into appropriate pairs. In response to Theseus's questioning, Lysander confesses that he and Hermia have fled from the city specifically to escape the authority of the Athenian law (IV.1.150–152). Egeus bursts in, interrupting Lysander, with a speech stressing once again his *alazon* role, his determination to force his own choice of marriage partner upon his daughter, and his reliance upon the law to authorise his tyranny:

Enough, enough — my lord, you have enough!
I beg the law, the law upon his head.

> They would have stolen away, they would, Demetrius,
> Thereby to have defeated you and me —
> You of your wife, and me of my consent —
> Of my consent that she should be your wife.
>
> (IV.1.153–158)

This is typical *alazon* bluster, but it is also, as it turns out, Egeus's last speech in the play. Theseus, the good ruler who earlier had stressed his responsibility to uphold the letter of the law in telling Hermia that 'by no means' could he soften the rigour of the statute condemning her to death or perpetual chastity, now does precisely this:

> Egeus, I will overbear your will;
> For in the temple by and by with us
> These couples shall eternally be knit.
>
> (IV.1.178–180)

Like the blustering Egeus, the law itself is reduced to silence, and this suggests that Athens itself is now a different kind of place, its ruler no longer at the service of a repressive older order identified with sterility and death, but now the champion of youth, festivity and love.

Act V of *A Midsummer Night's Dream* is devoted to revelry and is set in the period between the performance of the multiple-marriage ceremony and the withdrawal of the newly-weds to bed. This highly charged interval is taken up with the performance of a play and concludes with a dance, after which Theseus leads the lovers off to consummate, and so to complete, their marriages:

> The iron tongue of midnight hath told twelve.
> Lovers, to bed; 'tis almost fairy time.
>
> (V.1.353–354)

But the play isn't yet quite over. Puck enters, followed by Oberon and Titania 'with all their train', and Oberon is given a speech in which he instructs his followers to range through the house and to 'bless' with consecrated dew 'each several chamber ... with sweet peace' (V.1.405–408).

> Now until the break of day
> Through this house each fairy stray.

To the best bride bed will we,
Which by us shall blessèd be;
And the issue there create
Ever shall be fortunate.

(V.1.391–396)

This comedy ends literally, as so many comedies end symbolically, with the creation of new life. Death, barrenness and hate have been defeated by life, fertility and love, just as each year the harsh and sterile grip of winter yields at last to the green renewal of spring.

What is it, in *A Midsummer Night's Dream*, that allows this transformation to take place? The answer, of course, is to be found in the events that occur in the mysterious wood near Athens where the main action of the comedy is set. The wood is just the kind of topsy-turvy world that comedy so often presents us with; the mortals who venture into it are swept up in a head-spinning whirl of upheavals and reversals, the playthings of mysterious forces of whose very existence they are unaware. Presiding gleefully over all this chaos is Puck the *bomolochos*, a capricious lord of misrule whose delight is in absurdity and whose very essence is mischievousness ('. . . those things do best please me/ That befall preposterously', III.2.120–121), but who is also able to reassure us — at the moment when the confusion is at its height — that the happy ending we desire will come to pass: 'Jack shall have Jill;/ Naught shall go ill' (III.2.461–462).

The wood is a *natural* place, unlike the man-made city where Theseus's court is located. It is governed by the fairies, who are intimately connected with nature; we learn from Titania that her quarrel with Oberon has caused profound disturbance in the natural world (II.1.88–117), and she tells Bottom that summer itself waits in attendance on her (III.1.146). These nature spirits, moreover, are well disposed toward mortals. Puck is a mischief-maker, it is true, but he is finally under the control of Oberon who, like Titania, has come to bless Theseus's marriage; we note that when Oberon first observes Helena in trouble, he immediately wants to help her (II.1.245–246, 259–266). The wood seems to be dangerous and frightening, and is certainly mysterious, but it turns out to be a benign and healing world where confusion leads to the discovery of true identity and where hatred turns to love — Theseus enters its outskirts and at once becomes able to nullify the bitter law of civilised Athens. All the mortal characters go back to the court in the end — it is their world, after all — but the Athens to which they return is a different and better place than the city from which Hermia and Lysander had fled at the end of Act I.

The transformation has been brought about by the experiences of the mortal characters in a world of pure comedy, a world free from the restraining limits of everyday order and everyday logic, where anything can happen and nothing is as it seems. Hermia and Lysander wish to escape from the rules of a society that seeks to regulate their desires and has the power to do so; they find refuge in a fertile natural world which confuses and frightens at first but which turns out to be friendly to their wishes and capable of realising them. Like the young lovers in *A Midsummer Night's Dream*, we the audience live in a world where our desires are circumscribed by a complex network of customs and laws, both man-made and physical. This is as it must be — it is the price we pay for living in the real world and for the protection and support that living in society offers us — but it means that many things that we would find profoundly desirable are denied to us. We cannot, like Hermia and Lysander, find a magic wood and as a result of what happens there achieve the happy ending of our desires. But for a couple of hours we can share imaginatively in such a world, where anything is possible and where everything is guaranteed to turn out all right. It is this imaginative release from order, rule and duty into a realm of playfulness, freedom and hope that *A Midsummer Night's Dream* offers us. We all need a holiday from reality from time to time, an escape from our deep knowledge that we have to behave ourselves and that, even if we do, we must still grow old and die. Comedy offers us just such a holiday, a vision of absolute freedom ending in the promise of living happily ever after. This is why people have made and delighted in comedies for as long as we can tell, and why the ancient patterns of comedy will endure.

AFTERTHOUGHTS

1

Explain the relevance to Treadwell's argument of his opening account of conventions of early comedies (20–23).

2

How important is fertility (see page 25) in *A Midsummer Night's Dream* as a whole?

3

Do you agree that the wood in *A Midsummer Night's Dream* is ultimately 'a benign and healing world' (page 27)?

4

What attitude is taken in this essay towards laws ('both man-made and physical')?

Ronald Draper

*Ronald Draper is Regius Professor of
Literature at the University of Aberdeen,
and the author of numerous scholarly
publications.*

ESSAY

Appearance and reality in *A Midsummer Night's Dream*

The very title of *A Midsummer Night's Dream* indicates its unreality. The whole thing is an artificial performance, the deliberate creating of a series of illusions for the purpose of entertainment by men and boys whose profession it is to adopt the characters and guises of people that they are not. At the end, one of their number playing the part of Puck refers to himself and his fellow-actors as 'shadows' and invites the audience to treat the performance they have just witnessed as the equivalent of a dream:

> If we shadows have offended,
> Think but this, and all is mended:
> That you have but slumbered here
> While these visions did appear.
> And this weak and idle theme,
> No more yielding but a dream

(V.1.413–418)

Within the play itself there are characters, the Athenian

workmen — Peter Quince, Francis Flute, Tom Snout, Snug, Robin Starveling, and, above all, the egregious, self-satisfied, yet energetically irrepressible Bottom — who represent prosaically down-to-earth men of the ordinary day-to-day world; but at the other extreme there are supernatural beings like Oberon and Titania and their attendant fairies who possess magical powers, flit through the air with incredible speed, sing delicate lullabies, and can make fans from the wings of 'painted butterflies'. And these opposite extremes are brought into ludicrous union when Bottom, transformed into half-man, half-ass, becomes the love object of the doting Titania, who promises to 'purge thy mortal grossness so/ That thou shalt like an airy spirit go' (III.1.151–152). In between there are the lovers, Hermia, Helena, Lysander and Demetrius, who may seem to represent more normal human beings, but whose behaviour, when they enter the transmogrified, moonlit world of the woodlands outside Athens and are subjected to the strange effects of Puck's 'love-in-idleness', just as fully justifies Helena's prophetic declaration, in the opening scene, that:

> Things base and vile, holding no quantity,
> Love can transpose to form and dignity.
> Love looks not with the eyes, but with the mind,
> And therefore is winged Cupid painted blind.

> (I.1.232–235)

Only Theseus and Hippolyta seem able to keep appearance and reality in rational relation to each other. Theseus, indeed, in the much-quoted speech which opens Act V seems to signal a return to the sane, daylight world after so much that has been 'wood within this wood' (II.1.192), when, dismissing the lovers' tales as 'antique fables' and 'fairy toys', he goes on to analyse the illusions which possess the minds of lunatics, lovers and poets alike as the 'tricks' of 'strong' imagination, which 'if it would but apprehend some joy/ It comprehends some bringer of that joy', and concludes with an example of fearful appearance reduced to harmless reality, in a couplet of anti-romantic bathos:

> Or in the night, imagining some fear,
> How easy is a bush supposed a bear?

> (V.1.21–22)

Yet he also employs words within the body of the speech which, at least with regard to the poet, give imagination a very different dimension:

> The poet's eye, in a fine frenzy rolling,
> Doth glance from heaven to earth, from earth to heaven.
> And as imagination bodies forth
> The forms of things unknown, the poet's pen
> Turns them to shapes, and gives to airy nothing
> A local habitation and a name.
>
> (V.1.12–17)

This suggests both the astonishing range of the poet's imagination and its essentially creative — almost god-like — capacity to bring 'reality' into being from nothing. The words perhaps echo Sidney's famous defence of poetry as a medium for creating a 'golden' world which excels the real, or commonly recognised, world to which history and philosophy are confined; but if so, the 'local habitation and a name' with which such creatures of transcendent fantasy are said to be endowed seem to give them a solidity challenging that of the normally 'real'. At the very least, the separation of categories is broken down and there is a sense of reality as multiple in its levels.

More specifically this is the effect created on the lovers by their experience in the wood. When they return to normality (in IV.1) they feel themselves to be in an in-between world:

> DEMETRIUS These things seem small and undistinguishable,
> Like far-off mountains turnèd into clouds.
> HERMIA Methinks I see these things with parted eye,
> When everything seems double.
> HELENA   So methinks,
> And I have found Demetrius, like a jewel,
> Mine own and not mine own.
> DEMETRIUS   Are you sure
> That we are awake? It seems to me
> That yet we sleep, we dream.
>
> (IV.1.186–193)

The figures here are those of simile and paradox, which seem to separate and distinguish, but do so only to merge and identify. Solid mountains turn into vaporous clouds; possessions are owned and not owned; single things are seen double; and sleeping and waking, seeing and dreaming, are perilously near to being equated.

Thus the very bases of normal experience are questioned in this play. Its presiding symbol is the moon — a planet that waxes and wanes, a by-word for mutability, and one that gives a pale, uncertain light. The moon is evoked in the first ten lines of the opening scene (and, paradoxically again, by the 'daylight' characters, Theseus and Hippolyta) in both negative and positive terms. Initially the moon is on the wane, as Theseus expresses his impatience for his wedding with Hippolyta and the night of its consummation. He is a young man eager to come into his inheritance, but prevented by a dowager-moon who still lives on to frustrate him. In four days' time, however, the old moon will complete its cycle; the replacement of Theseus's tawdry imagery by the beauty of Hippolyta's carries with it the implied renewal of the new moon, and a ritual splendour which is acted out in the formal repetition of the language:

> Four days will quickly steep themselves in night;
> Four nights will quickly dream away the time:
> And then the moon — like to a silver bow
> New-bent in heaven — shall behold the night
> Of our solemnities.

(I.1.7–11)

Such waning and waxing is also anticipatory of the play itself — and, as a further extension of meaning — of the nature of the comic genre to which it belongs. Concord grows out of discord, light comes out of dark, threats of sterility and death give way to reconciliation and rejoicing. But, as so often in Shakespearean comedy, the one does not completely wipe out the other; a mingled impression remains which, like the ambiguous quality of moonlight, teases and tantalises with images of a deliciously contradictory nature.

One way of reading A Midsummer Night's Dream is to see it as the triumph of common sense over irrationality, of the real over the illusory. On this interpretation the play begins with wilfulness on the part of Hermia and Lysander, determined to run away from Athens, and equal wilfulness on the part of Egeus, determined to assert his parental authority, with little regard, it seems, for the feelings of his daughter. Will rather than reason likewise determines Demetrius's infatuation with Hermia, for whom he has deserted the doting Helena — herself another victim of the irrational in her obsession with a faithless lover. Love's encouragement of irrationality is further illustrated by the Bottom/Titania story, and its arbitrariness is exemplified by Oberon's use of the flower, love-in-idleness, to dupe not only Titania but also Demetrius and Lysander. The latter's claim in II.2 that his desertion of Hermia for Helena is dictated by reason (lines 121–128) serves only to emphasise the illusion to which he is subjected; while Bottom's cheerful response to Titania's declaration of love, 'to say the truth, reason and love keep little company together nowadays' (III.1.136–137), is the fool's unwittingly wise comment on what is indeed the truth of his situation and that of the lovers, too. Finally, daylight and emergence from the wood of error signify the restoration of reason and order, with the triple weddings of Theseus/Hippolyta, Lysander/Hermia and Demetrius/Helena putting the seal to comedy's destined happy ending.

Clearly, such a view has its validity. It is one of the levels on which the play operates. But to offer it as *the* interpretation is reductive. Shakespeare's imagination embraces so much more, and the world of *A Midsummer Night's Dream* is both more discriminating and more tolerant. This is especially evident in regard to the presentation of the fairies and, at the other extreme, the character of Bottom.

The first appearance of the fairies is in Act II scene 1, coinciding with the shifting of the scene of action from Athens to the wood. Puck asks an unnamed Fairy, 'Whither wander you?'; and the Fairy replies in verse which not only, as Stanley Wells comments in the Penguin edition (Commentary, p. 131), 'forms an immediate contrast with the mechanicals' prose' (of I.2), but which also differs in its two-stress, then four-stress, lines from any of the five-stress, rhymed or unrhymed, lines so far used. Its pace is trippingly rapid and it gives expression both in form and content to a freedom of movement and relationship with nature entirely unprecedented:

> Over hill, over dale,
>> Thorough bush, thorough briar,
> Over park, over pale,

Thorough flood, thorough fire —
I do wander everywhere
Swifter than the moon's sphere,
And I serve the Fairy Queen,
To dew her orbs upon the green.
The cowslips tall her pensioners be;
In their gold coats spots you see —
Those be rubies, fairy favours;
In those freckles live their savours.

(II.1.2–13)

The picture this paints is of a creature who is released from normal human limitations, and of a natural world which is alive with personified beings. Dewdrops and cowslips become part of a strange, new fairy activity that quite transforms the ordinary human perception of them; they belong to a heightened version of reality which is breathtakingly revealed as existing behind what we take to be a commonplace surface. The film of familiarity is stripped away, and we enter a new world.

There is, of course, a risk of what is created in this fairy dimension seeming whimsical and prettified. Many a school play production of *A Midsummer Night's Dream* falls hopelessly into this trap, especially, for example, in the scene of Titania's summoning her fairy attendants to 'kill cankers in the muskrose buds' and 'war with reremice for their leathern wings' (II.2.3–4), then falling asleep soothed by fairy lullabies. It was no doubt to avoid the sugariness such passages can be easily distorted into (but it *is* distortion) that Peter Brook produced his notorious urchin fairies who looked more like Golding's *Lord of the Flies* children in an advanced state of regression to primitive behaviour. But Shakespeare provides his own corrective by the different insight he gives us into fairy power when the quarrel between Oberon and Titania is evocatively presented as the source of natural 'distemperature' which amounts almost to chaos:

The spring, the summer,
The childing autumn, angry winter change
Their wonted liveries and the mazèd world
By their increase now knows not which is which.

(II.1.111–114)

It is a 'progeny of evils' of which the King and Queen of fairies are the 'parents and original' (II.1.81–117). Oberon is 'King of shadows' (III.2.347) and can command Puck to cover 'the starry welkin' with 'drooping fog as black as Acheron' (III.2.356–357), though he and Titania are not to be equated with 'damned spirits' which must troop back to their graves with the coming of light (379–387). 'But we are spirits of another sort,' he boasts, and he claims that he himself has the privilege of being companion to Aurora, in verse that creates a glowingly golden image of the dawn:

> I with the morning's love have oft made sport,
> And like a forester the groves may tread
> Even till the eastern gate all fiery red
> Opening on Neptune with fair blessèd beams
> Turns into yellow gold his salt green streams.
>
> (III.2.389–393)

Puck is Oberon's executant, but gives yet another dimension to fairy reality — a coarse, peasant, practical-joke-playing dimension. He manufactures illusions for the sake of broad farce (which, interestingly, forges a link with the 'rude mechanicals', instead of emphasising the contrast as the Titania/Bottom encounter does); and he tells of them with a deliberate relish for vulgar language:

> ... sometime lurk I in a gossip's bowl
> In very likeness of a roasted crab;
> And when she drinks, against her lips I bob,
> And on her withered dewlap pour the ale.
> The wisest aunt telling the saddest tale
> Sometime for threefoot stool mistaketh me;
> Then slip I from her bum.
>
> (II.1.47–53)

Collectively, these fairies have the variability of the play's pervasive moonlight; they cannot be confined to one character or one dimension only. At the end of the play they become beneficent spirits blessing the house of matrimony and warding off evil from what is the promise of further creativity in the form of the offspring yet to be begotten by the lovers who have retired to their beds to consummate their desire for each other. Nevertheless, they are destined to become, as we have already noted, mere 'shadows' dependent on the whim and favour of the audience. Their reality is as evanescent as the power of imagination itself; in some respects the most potent force in the play, it is also the most fragile.

Bottom and his companions, on the other hand, inhabit a one-dimensional world from which imagination, it seems, is comically entirely absent. They intend to grace Theseus's wedding night with a fictional entertainment, *'The most lamentable comedy and most cruel death of Pyramus and Thisbe'* (I.2.11–12), but their literal-mindedness shows that they have no conception of what fiction is. The tacit assumption made by all dramatists and performers that they share with their audience an understanding of the need to make illusion affectingly real, while never losing sight of its illusory nature, is a form of sophistication which eludes these innocent non-sophisticates completely.

It is Bottom who becomes the philosopher and critic of this unsophisticated world, voicing its ludicrously prosaic anxieties: 'There are things in this comedy of Pyramus and Thisbe that will never please,' he says. 'First, Pyramus must draw a sword to kill himself, which the ladies cannot abide' (III.1.8–10). The solution he propounds is to write a prologue explaining that Pyramus is not really killed and that 'Pyramus' is not really Pyramus, but himself, Bottom the weaver. This is childish, but also less than childish, for the conventions of make-believe are well understood by story-loving and play-making children. Imagination is strong in them, endowing the simplest properties with imaginary qualities, and allowing acts of 'violence' to be committed which are nothing but ritualised gestures. Bottom might, of course, be justified in his concern for the ladies in his potential audience if his company's acting powers and physical resources permitted them to create a totally convincing illusion (though that would also be to disregard all the assumptions that are made when the context is a place of, and occasion for, entertainment), but what adds to the farcical pleasure of the spectacle is the woodenness of the play's verse and the sheer banality of its language, together with the utter remoteness of Bottom's own acting style ('Ercles' vein') from anything likely to be thought real. He is thus doubly — and from the actual theatre audience's point of view, delightfully — innocent of the relationship between illusion and reality on which dramatic presentation depends. He understands neither its conventional nature nor the mimetic conventions which might conceivably lead to the disturbing realism he fears.

Other ludicrous devices follow: an actor-lion who lets half his face be seen through the lion's neck; a man-in-the-moon with a bush of thorns and a lantern, to represent Moonshine; and a man with 'some roughcast' about him to signify Wall, with fingers crooked to make a cranny to whisper through. All these are logical consequences of the same wonderful ignorance of the way drama depends on the audience's ability to distinguish between appearance and reality even while allowing themselves to take the appearance for real. Yet, curiously, this literalism of the 'rude mechanicals' complements the daring imaginative flights which the play of *A Midsummer Night's Dream* itself takes, for example, with the fairies. The comedy thus provokes the tendency to laugh at the workmen's naïvety, encourages sympathetic acceptance of the perhaps extravagant illusions which the play creates, and thus opens up possibilities of an altogether richer complexity.

At the same time Bottom in particular becomes a great comic asset in welding together the prose and poetry in this play. The ease and readiness with which he accepts Titania's devotion and the service of her fairies in IV.1 may from one point of view seem like egregious egoism on his part, but from another they show him to have an admirable capacity to adapt to new circumstances and an authority, combined with a kind of innate courtesy in the handling of servants, which, notwithstanding the differences of rank and class, would be worthy of Duke Theseus. And when Bottom is wakened to normal reality and returned to his proper human shape, his ingenuity in devising a means of making capital out of his 'dream' is equally impressive. In his excitement and temporary bewilderment he makes a farcical muddle of the relation between the five senses (and manages to garble a famous passage from 1 Corinthians 2:9 as well): 'The eye of man hath not heard, the ear of man hath not seen, man's hand is not able to taste, his tongue to conceive, nor his heart to report what my dream was!' (IV.1.208–211). Yet this very confusion, following as it does on the lovers' bewilderment as they also make the transition from dream to reality, not only increases the impression that an experience has been undergone which cannot be expressed in the usual language of rationality, but also heightens the sense of the rapidity and ease with which Bottom can switch from one state of mind of another. From astonishment at his own 'most rare vision' he leaps, almost with agility, to the idea of having Peter Quince turn it into a ballad, which he then ingeniously proposes to use as part of the forthcoming wedding entertainment. And then, with an egotism which is little short of brilliant, he sees himself as the glorious centrepiece of the whole performance: 'Peradventure, to make it the more gracious I shall sing it at her death' (lines 15–16). This is both ridiculously inappropriate and amusingly inventive at the same time; and it is further evidence of Bottom's nimble capacity to move from one level of reality to another with complete freedom, and no feeling of embarrassment whatever.

None of this is meant to suggest that Bottom should be presented as a character who is conscious of the way such interaction between different levels of reality takes place. His role as comic butt would be radically changed if this were so; and the uproariously farcical humour of his unwilling participation in the trick played on Titania, and only too willing participation in the farcical tragedy of *Pyramus and Thisbe*, would be quite subverted. He is, and must remain, sublimely unaware of what he is doing, and what is being done to him. It is only from the audience's privileged position that he and his fellow-workmen can be seen as contributors to this process of complicating the relationship between appearance and reality.

For that matter, none of the characters within the play, with the possible — and even then, very limited — exceptions of Theseus and Oberon, is to be understood as possessing any such degree of self-consciousness. Shakespeare is not concerned here, as it might be argued that he is in the later tragedies, with awareness of the conflicting or interacting relations between appearance and reality in the mind of a particular character within the play, but with the play as a means of exploring the nature of those relations and, in the process, dilating the audience's awareness of them. He is also concerned — indeed, perhaps it should be said that he is first and foremost concerned — with providing entertainment for his audience. But these two statements are not incompatible, for it is through the comic collisions created by deceptive appearances and the farcical effects created by characters who both underestimate and over-estimate the nature of the dramatic illusion itself that the excitement and amusement of the audience are aroused. The imaginative dimension which can 'body forth the forms of things unknown' is likewise an essential part of this process.

The 'reality' of such a dramatic entertainment as *A Midsummer Night's Dream* is thus a complex matter of illusion created by the interplay of words and actions (and to some extent musical effects as well) which do not simply mime the appearances of a recognisably common-sense world, but also extend the audience's response beyond that world into a romantic realm of heightened feeling — feeling experienced by both human and non-human dramatis personae, both lovers and fairies, and set against a natural world which is itself imaginatively approximated to the human by a beautiful, vitalising rhetoric of personification. This, together with anti-romantic debunking of appearances, and a prosaically naïve failure on the part of Bottom and Co. to understand the very meaning of appearance and reality, is what the rich texture of the play is composed of, giving its 'weak and idle theme' the paradoxically dream-like strength of vision. It is not simply a comedy of appearance *versus* reality, but of appearance and reality teasingly, and yet fascinatingly, intermingled. What seems, and what is, can no longer be distinguished, for all is 'shadow' attending on the good will of the viewer.

AFTERTHOUGHTS

1

Do you agree that 'Only Theseus and Hippolyta seem able to keep appearance and reality in rational relation to each other' (page 31)?

2

Does Draper persuade you that 'the very bases of normal experience are questioned in this play' (page 33)?

3

How 'young' (page 33) do you imagine Theseus to be?

4

Explain the significance of Bottom (pages 38–39) to Draper's argument that *A Midsummer Night's Dream* is 'not simply a comedy of appearance *versus* reality, but of appearances and reality teasingly, and yet fascinatingly, intermingled' (page 40).

Cedric Watts

Cedric Watts is Professor of English at Sussex University, and the author of many scholarly publications.

ESSAY

The translation of Bottom

This essay has two parts, Part 1 is about the word 'translation', and Part 2 is about Bottom's relationship with Titania.

1

'Bless thee, Bottom! Bless thee! Thou art translated!' (III.1.112–113). So says Quince, soon after Bottom has unwittingly had his head converted by Puck into that of an ass. 'Translated' means literally 'carried across' (from Latin, *trans*, across, and *latum*, carried). Bottom undergoes a translation in the sense of a physical transformation. It is also, in part, a psychological transformation: for, though he retains most of his normal personality (complacent, resilient, resourceful), he acquires some of the desires of the animal: he will hunger for hay and relish a scratching. In addition, he undergoes a translation in a different sense: the metaphorical is translated into the literal. He is, metaphorically, something of an ass in his naïvety and stubbornness, and now the partial likeness is rendered literal as his head is transformed into an ass's. 'Translated' can mean 'transferred' (often from a lower state to a higher), as in the biblical phrasing, 'God ... hath delivered us from the power of darkness, and hath translated us into the kingdom of his dear Son';[1] and Bottom is translated in this sense when he is borne away by his entranced lover, Titania. A translator (at a conference, say) is an interpreter; and in this essay I shall attempt the translation of Bottom, in the sense that I shall interpret his transformation and transference; so I offer a translation of his translations.

One of the basic reasons for Shakespeare's poetic and dramatic power is his ability to interrelate the abstract and the concrete. His schooling in Latin had given him a Latin subconscious mind, so that words which to a less educated mind would seem simply abstract were readily convertible by him into their very specific components. The urge to interrelate abstract and concrete, testing one against the other, is one of the motivating forces of a dramatist: Shakespeare renders a story (with its themes, moral lessons, ideological implications) concrete and specific by converting it into a drama to be enacted on a public stage by living people. His translatory imagination extends into numerous features of his plays. For instance, *Troilus and Cressida* deals with the Trojan war, and the play suggests that the war is rotten at its centre, for the beautiful Helen, an adulteress, is not worth all the bloodshed that her abduction has caused. At the height of the battle, Hector pursues an opponent who wears 'sumptuous armour'; he kills him, opens the armour, and finds 'a putrefièd core' (a rotten corpse or putrefied centre) inside. So the notion of a war which is rotten at its core is translated into a physical, visual symbol. Again, *Troilus and Cressida* and *King Lear* deploy the idea that evil is eventually self-destructive, since wicked people eventually turn against other wicked people. As Ulysses puts it in *Troilus and Cressida*:

> . . . appetite, an universal wolf,
> So doubly seconded with will and power,
> Must make perforce an universal prey,
> And last eat up himself.[2]

(I.3.121–124)

---

[1] Colossians 1:10, 13.
[2] Quotation from *The Complete Works*, edited by Peter Alexander (London and Glasgow, 1951).

This idea, of evil or egoistic appetite as cannibalistic and self-destructive, had been translated by Shakespeare into grossly physical terms in his very first tragedy, *Titus Andronicus*, when Tamora, the wicked queen, literally eats the flesh of her evil sons.

A Midsummer Night's Dream is a delightful fantasia, combining lyricism, farcical comedy, ludicrous confusions, arcadian festivity, interpenetrating hierarchies of beings, and intermingled dimensions of legend, folklore and everyday rustic life. Its pleasures are largely escapist pleasures; audiences enjoy an imaginative holiday from sober, sombre actualities. Yet its staying-power as a drama depends also on its underlying human realities. That a weaver should magically have his head transformed into an ass's is fantastic; yet the fantasy has its underlying logic: Bottom's partly asinine character is rendered in physical terms. Then Titania, under the influence of the magic charm derived from the flower 'love-in-idleness' (the pansy), absurdly falls in love with him. Yet the comedy of her infatuation with an ass-headed weaver still relates to familiar realities; and Bottom himself has the sense to recognise some of them. Titania, entranced, says:

> Mine ear is much enamoured of thy note.
> So is mine eye enthrallèd to thy shape,
> And thy fair virtue's force perforce doth move me
> On the first view to say, to swear, I love thee.
>
> (III.1.131–134)

Bottom reasonably replies:

> Methinks, mistress, you should have little reason for that. And yet, to say the truth, reason and love keep little company together nowadays
>
> (III.1.135–137)

What the love of Titania for Bottom displays in farcically parodic and overt form is a range of commonplaces: love is blind; or, love overcomes sober judgement; or, love beautifies its object. At a wedding recently, a woman behind me said, after looking critically at the bridegroom, 'I wonder what she sees in him?' Such comments have been made at weddings down the centuries; and *A Midsummer Night's Dream*, which, almost certainly, was written to form part of the marriage festivities uniting two noble families,[3] celebrates love which leads to marriage while first offering comic demonstrations of love's transformative powers. In accelerated, heightened form, the play deals with some very familiar and perennial facts: not only that amatory desire imparts beauty to the ugly, but also that lovers promise constancy while often proving inconstant; that sexuality drives the socially high and low alike; that sexual desire is at once comically humiliating, lyrically exalting, and biologically essential for human survival.

2

Titania takes Bottom away to her bower. Are we to imagine that they actually copulate? Professor Harold F Brooks, editor of the Arden text of the play, says:

> even a controlled suggestion of carnal bestiality is surely impossible; jealous Oberon will not have cast a spell to cuckold himself. Her dotage is imaginative and emotional.

The editor's phrase, 'carnal bestiality', seems unfairly prejudicial, since what is at issue is simply the possibility of sexual intercourse between man and woman. Bottom wears an ass's head, but his body remains that of a man; and the entranced Titania sees him not as beast but as 'gentle mortal'. 'Jealous Oberon will not have cast a spell to cuckold himself,' says the editor: well, Oberon will not have intended such an outcome, but it makes the play funnier and actually morally better if he *is* cuckolded, since his own conduct is morally suspect. Titania has been infatuated with a 'changeling boy'; Oberon, jealous, demands that the boy should become 'Knight of his train, to trace the forests wild' (II.1.25); and eventually, while she is still subject to the magic of love-in-idleness, Oberon taunts her and makes her agree to hand over the child. He thus wins this bizarre 'tug-of-love' dispute by taking advantage of Titania's

---

[3] Probably the wedding of Elizabeth, the daughter of Sir George Carey, to Thomas, the son of Henry, Lord Berkeley, on 19 February 1596.

bewitched state. If, in the meantime, he has been unwittingly cuckolded, that perhaps serves him right for having acted mischievously and bullyingly. We know that his schemes *can* miscarry: his plan to reconcile Demetrius and Helena went wildly wrong as a result of Puck's mismanagement. So perhaps he deserves to be fooled by the outcome of the meeting of Titania and Bottom.

The most celebrated modern production of the play, by Peter Brook (Royal Shakespeare Company, 1970), certainly suggested that Bottom's translation is, among other things, translation to a realm of sexual bliss with Titania. Much of the action of that production took place in an austerely white setting, a kind of gymnasium with climbing-frames; when Oberon talked to Puck, the two sat on trapezes which swung to and fro, over the stage and out over the orchestra-pit. In contrast to this austerity, when Titania conveyed Bottom away, Bottom joined her triumphantly in a vast crimson bed, like a huge nest of bright feathers; the bed ascended heavenwards, and, as it did, so, the stage erupted into festivity and wild noise: a jazz band played while rejoicing figures scattered streamers into the audience. Brook's production was influenced by the Japanese theatre and by circuses featuring acrobats and gymnasts; but probably the biggest influence was the 'permissive' spirit of those times, and the heart of the play, in that version, was the sense of sexual joy as Bottom and Titania embraced. One obvious fault, though, was that Bottom wore no ass-head, merely a clown's red nose and a cap whose flaps vaguely suggested long ears. This contradicted the text, which specifies a hairy ass's head, and accordingly reduced the absurd comedy and muffled the theme of love's blindness.

The most enjoyable production of *A Midsummer Night's Dream* that I've seen was not Peter Brook's but a local production with amateur performers. It took place in a Sussex village a few years ago; the location was the garden of Rudyard Kipling's former house; the walls, trees and bushes of the garden sufficed as scenery; and the audience consisted not of academics and students but of the local village-people who turned out with picnic hampers and bottles of wine to enjoy the evening. Bottom, played magnificently by a Mr Ken Spalding, wore a realistic ass's head with ears operated (apparently) by concealed strings, so that when Titania declared her love for him, the ears grew instantly erect, implying both astonishment and a possibly sexual excitement. By gesture and intonation, this actor strongly suggested that his abduction by Titania had its sexual consequence. Up to a point, this is in harmony with the text. Consider what Titania says at the end of Act III scene 1:

> Come, wait upon him. Lead him to my bower.
> The moon methinks looks with a watery eye;
> And when she weeps, weeps every little flower,
> Lamenting some enforcèd chastity.
> Tie up my lover's tongue; bring him silently.
>
> (III.1.192–196)

The comedy here clearly lies in the vocal counterpoint between Titania's lyricism and Bottom's inarticulate asinine half-braying sounds, as well as in the visual contrast between the regal beauty of Titania and the ludicrous clumsiness of an ass-headed weaver. At the words 'Lamenting some enforcèd chastity', Bottom made noises expressive of consternation (implying, hilariously, his apprehension of being forcibly 'deflowered' by her); and some such comical noises were probably intended by Shakespeare, otherwise there would be far less point in the line 'Tie up my lover's tongue; bring him silently'. What's more, the linkage of 'enforcèd chastity' with 'Tie up my lover's tongue' connects the notion of enforcement with Bottom. At Act IV scene 1, when Bottom and Titania reappear, it is clear that in the interim their union has been entirely happy and fulfilling; Bottom is now relaxed and at ease, ready for food and sleep, while Titania lovingly embraces him. They resemble a slightly absurd, intoxicated yet gratified, honeymoon couple. So the notion of an unwittingly cuckolded Oberon has some support in the text; and, indeed, it has been heralded by the song from Bottom that had first awakened the enchanted Titania:

> The finch, the sparrow, and the lark,
> The plainsong cuckoo grey,
> Whose note full many a man doth mark
> And dares not answer 'Nay'
>
> (III.1.123–126)

(By singing 'Cuckoo, cuckoo', the bird reminds married men of the possibility that they may be cuckolded; for, as the cuckoo's offspring is unsuspectingly reared by another bird, so the cuckolded husband may unsuspectingly rear another man's offspring.) If I am right, however, Bottom has been translated not only to a region of sexual bliss but also to one refined and spiritualised by magic and fantasy. Titania had promised: 'I will purge thy mortal grossness so/ That thou shalt like an airy spirit go' (III.1.151–152). (In Milton's *Paradise Lost*, the archangel Raphael explains to Adam that when spirits embrace, a perfect merging ensues: 'Total they mix' and 'obstacle find none/ Of membrane, joint, or limb'.) Furthermore, the subsequent dialogues of Bottom with Peaseblossom, Cobweb, Moth and Mustardseed (the fairies being traditionally played by young children) give a quality of childish innocence and fairy-tale fantasy to the situation. What is implied is a translation into a transcendent realm of dream-like experience; at the centre of it may be a sexual embrace, but one rendered both innocent and, eventually, ineffable. By 'ineffable' I mean 'beyond expression'; for that is what Bottom later finds to be the case.

> I have had a most rare vision. I have had a dream past the wit of man to say what dream it was. Man is but an ass if he go about to expound this dream. Methought I was — there is no man can tell what. Methought I was — and methought I had — but man is but a patched fool if he will offer to say what methought I had.
>
> (IV.1.203–208)

Well, this 'patched fool', Cedric Watts, will offer to say that Bottom and Titania, though they soon forget their union, have actually made fools of Puck and Oberon.

Shakespeare was no socialist. In his plays, the common people, shepherds, rustics, carpenters, tinkers, tailors and the like, tend to figure as buffoons and simpletons. Near the end of the play, Bottom and his friends perform *Pyramus and Thisbe*, and their performance of this 'tragedy' becomes a predictably ludicrous fiasco. Meanwhile, Oberon and Titania are reconciled; Theseus is to marry Hippolyta; Hermia will wed Lysander, while Helena weds Demetrius. Hierarchic, aristocratic notions of social order are flatteringly endorsed. But morally and socially, one of the most satisfactory features of the play is that the most ineffable sexual experience, one transcending words, one eluding translation into ordinary terminology, has been the experience of the transformed Bottom and the entranced Titania. It provides the concealed but tantalising centre of the whole drama. I have argued that the lyrical fantasia which is *A Midsummer Night's Dream* has an underlying strength which derives from its readiness to translate into graphic images and memorable poetry some familiar emotional commonplaces. What Bottom's brief honeymoon with Titania expresses is a combination of several such commonplaces. First, that sexual love can make bedfellows of most unlikely partners; second, that while, to outsiders, it may seem childish or ludicrous, such love can at best reconcile 'mortal grossness' with experience which resembles enchantment and eludes the grasp of language. Bottom says that his experience should be called 'Bottom's Dream', 'because it hath no bottom' — suggesting both that it has no solid foundation and that it is unfathomably profound. His name means 'skein of thread' (obviously appropriate to a weaver) as well as 'buttocks'; and it suggests social lowliness. 'Titania' was one of the ancient names of Circe, the seductive enchantress, and of Selene or Diana, goddess of the moon; and, as commentators have often pointed out, imagery of the moon proliferates in this play, for that planet is associated with change, femininity, chastity, but also procreation: the moon goddess is tutelary deity of 'translation'. The union of Bottom with Titania (a partly burlesque counterpart of the legend of Endymion and Selene)[4] is a union of mortal with immortal, and of the socially low with the supernaturally high. Sexual love can, it appears, give fleeting intimations of immortality, even if such intimations prove no more durable than a dream.

Tedious realism reports the familiar; interesting realism surprises us into fresh appreciation of the familiar. The appeal of *A Midsummer Night's Dream* is largely escapist, for we enter a realm of folk-lore, fantasy, fairy-tale, romantic comedy and festive saturnalia. Yet, obliquely, glancingly, it invokes realities; it can still surprise us into recognition of what we have often sensed but seldom fully appraised.

---

[4] Endymion was a beautiful shepherd with whom the moon goddess Selene (or Diana) copulated nocturnally as he slept. Bottom's less illustrious ancestors include the hero of Apuleius's bawdy novel, *The Golden Ass*.

AFTERTHOUGHTS

1

What connotations of the word 'translation' are explored in this essay?

2

Do you prefer to think that Oberon was or wasn't cuckolded by Bottom and Titania?

3

Do you agree with Watts's comment that 'Shakespeare was no socialist' (page 48)?

4

What 'realities' (page 49) does *A Midsummer Night's Dream* invoke for you?

Michael Gearin-Tosh

Michael Gearin-Tosh is Fellow and Tutor in English Literature at St Catherine's College, Oxford. He is also Associate Director of the Oxford School of Drama.

ESSAY

The World of *A Midsummer Night's* Dream

A Midsummer Night's Dream is the only comedy by Shakespeare which contains grand characters from ancient myth and history. Theseus and Hippolyta are exotic by any standard, yet Shakespeare intensifies this otherness by placing them in a world of strange ritual, which we encounter as soon as the play opens:

> THESEUS Now, fair Hippolyta, our nuptial hour
> Draws on apace. Four happy days bring in
> Another moon — but O, methinks how slow
> This old moon wanes! She lingers my desires,
> Like to a stepdame or a dowager
> Long withering out a young man's revenue.
> HIPPOLYTA Four days will quickly steep themselves in night;
> Four nights will quickly dream away the time:
> And then the moon — like to a silver bow
> New-bent in heaven — shall behold the night
> Of our solemnities.
>
> (I.1.1–11)

This high reverence for the moon is grave and mysterious. In the next line Theseus summons Philostrate. He is not an important character but his name points to the link between *A Midsummer Night's Dream* and Chaucer's *The Knight's Tale* in which Theseus also presides over an adventure of love and in a setting of exotic richness.

One of the contending lovers, Arcite, is accompanied by the King of India:

> With Arcita, in stories as men fynde,
> The grete Emetreus, the kyng of Inde,
> Upon a steede bay trapped in steel,
> Covered in clooth of gold, dyapred weel,
> Cam ridynge lyk the god of armes, Mars.
> His cote-armure was of clooth of Tars
> Couched with perles white and rounde and grete;
> His sadel was of brend gold newe ybete;
> A mantelet upon his shulder hangynge,
> Bret-ful of rubyes rede as fyr sparklynge;
> His crispe heer lyk rynges was yronne,
> And that was yelow, and glytered as the sonne
> . . .
> Upon his hand he bar for his deduyt
> An egle tame, as any lilye whyt.
> . . .
> Aboute this kyng ther ran on every part
> Ful many a tame leon and leopart.
> And in this wise thise lordes, alle and some,
> Been on the Sonday to the citee come[1]
>
> (*The Knight's Tale*, I,11.2155–66, 2177–78, 2185–88)

This is a delighted catalogue of opulence. The king's clothes shine with pearls and rubies. Did white eagles exist? Probably not. Some commentators infer that Chaucer meant a falcon. But it seems as likely that he was revelling in the exotic notion of a white eagle — and tamed too. A contemporary earl had brought home a leopard from the East and this had excited people in Chaucer's England. But troops of tame lions and leopards run-

---

[1] *The Canterbury Tales*, The Riverside Chaucer (Oxford, 1988).

ning about the king's horse are incomparably rich and strange.

This passage is also marvellous in its use of colour. In common with many great painters, Chaucer restricts his palette to a dominant range of tone, in this case yellow, with areas of contrast. Set off by the rubies, pearls and eagle — the last two challenging each other in shades of white — the cloth of gold glistens under the saddle of 'brend gold new ybete' and the king's hair is like sunlight and shines against the yellows of the lions and leopards. There is a sumptuous pervading radiance which is never a monotone and moves between different shades into climaxes of brilliance.

A Midsummer Night's Dream is also a play of opulent speeches, yet its richness is of a fundamentally different kind:

> OBERON My gentle Puck, come hither. Thou rememberest
> Since once I sat upon a promontory,
> And heard a mermaid on a dolphin's back
> Uttering such dulcet and harmonious breath
> That the rude sea grew civil at her song,
> And certain stars shot madly from their spheres
> To hear the sea-maid's music?
> PUCK   I remember.
> OBERON That very time I saw — but thou couldst not
> Flying between the cold moon and the earth —
> Cupid all armed. A certain aim he took
> At a fair vestal thronèd by the west,
> And loosed his loveshaft smartly from his bow
> As it should pierce a hundred thousand hearts;
> But I might see young Cupid's fiery shaft
> Quenched in the chaste beams of the watery moon,
> And the imperial votaress passed on
> In maiden meditation, fancy-free.

(II.1.148–164)

There are no colours here, except in the fire of Cupid's shaft (and the little flower which follows these lines). Yet this speech describes mythological or mythic occurrences of a most heightened kind: a mermaid who disrupts the heavens, Cupid in person — Chaucer's king of India was only *like* Mars — and the moon extinguishing Cupid's shaft, as might occur in science fiction. Instead of colour, Shakespeare begins his effect with sound. The mermaid's song is heard against the swell of the sea which is declining. Then there are sights in the night sky, the wild movement of the stars followed by a drama which only Oberon can see. The visual incapacity of Puck is important: we share it and this prepares us to enter a world beyond that of ordinary perception.

The moon is never mentioned in *The Knight's Tale* although parts of the story take place at night. In contrast, the moon pervades *A Midsummer Night's Dream* right through to the comic man in the moon with his thornbush and dog in the play of the rude mechanicals — and finally in the last appearance of the fairies:

> PUCK   Now the hungry lion roars
> And the wolf behowls the moon
>
> . . .
>
> And we fairies, that do run
> By the triple Hecate's team,
> From the presence of the sun
> Following darkness like a dream,
> Now are frolic.

> (V.1.361–362, 373–377)

In these lines Hecate is the moon, Cynthia, drawn by her team of dragons.

The Knight's Tale is like a sumptuous tapestry but Shakespeare's descriptions are bleached of colour. His purpose is to give substance to this world of darkness and the moon. It is a world of sound and smell. Even the play's famous description of flowers avoids colour, which is extraordinary for a virtuoso speech on this subject:

> OBERON   I know a bank where the wild thyme blows,
> Where oxlips and the nodding violet grows,
> Quite overcanopied with luscious woodbine,
> With sweet muskroses and with eglantine;

> (II.1.249–252)

Perfume moves in the air from the thyme on the ground to the woodbine and muskroses above: 'luscious' was a word of scent as is 'sweet'. I am not arguing that there are never any colours but that it is remarkable how Shakespeare, in view of the opulence of his subject-matter, has curbed this tool of expression which he could use with such mastery. It is a sign of his earnestness in creating a world which is not our world, nor even the world of the mythological figures in the paintings of Titian and Poussin where gods and goddesses usually act out their dramas in meadows, woods and gardens which are lit by the sun.

This otherness is emphasised in the first scene. To Egeus, the world of moonlight is a place where illicit passions take over and disrupt what is good:

> This man hath bewitched the bosom of my child.
> Thou, thou, Lysander, thou hast given her rhymes,
> And interchanged love-tokens with my child.
> Thou hast by moonlight at her window sung
> With feigning voice verses of feigning love,
> And stolen the impression of her fantasy.
>
> (I.1.27–32)

To Theseus, it is the world of nuns who live in cold deprivation:

> For aye to be in shady cloister mewed,
> To live a barren sister all your life,
> Chanting faint hymns to the cold fruitless moon.
>
> (I.1.71–73)

Love, in contrast, revels in a world of colour:

> Your eyes are lodestars, and your tongue's sweet air
> More tuneable than lark to shepherd's ear
> When wheat is green, when hawthorn buds appear.
>
> (I.1.183–185)

The poetic climax of the first scene is the conclusion of the interchanges between Lysander and Hermia about the crosses of love. Lysander erupts with:

> Or if there were a sympathy in choice,
> War, death, or sickness did lay siege to it,
> Making it momentany as a sound,
> Swift as a shadow, short as any dream,
> Brief as the lightning in the collied night,
> That in a spleen, unfolds both heaven and earth,
> And — ere a man hath power to say 'Behold!' —

The jaws of darkness do devour it up.
So quick bright things come to confusion.

(I.1.141–149)

'Bright things' are extinguished in this world of night. Love is reduced to what is colourless, a shadow or a dream, and although the bright things of love are reasserted in Hermia's reply when she swears:

... by Cupid's strongest bow,
By his best arrow with the golden head,
...
And by that fire which burned the Carthage queen

(I.1.169–170, 173)

yet the ferocity of Lysander's outburst — the lightning in the collied night, and the jaws of darkness — is so potent that it jolts us. Can it be true?

As soon as the question is asked, we recall the opening of the scene and the:

... silver bow
New-bent in heaven ...

(lines 9–10)

Here is a bright thing which is not brought to confusion but instead presides over this world of night and hints at a mysterious underlying order. And the hint is carefully developed:

Four days will quickly steep themselves in night;
Four nights will quickly dream away the time:
And then the moon — like to a silver bow
New-bent in heaven — shall behold the night
Of our solemnities.

(lines 7–11)

For Hippolyta, night is not the enemy of day nor the sun hostile to the moon. The days seem to welcome night so that they may 'steep', a word of quiet luxury. And the 'bow/ New-bent' associates the moon with a fertility we more easily connect with the sun, its shape full of symbolism which is more commonly linked with Cupid's bow. Yet there is a subtle difference between them. Cupid's bow is unrecognisable without his arrow, his 'fiery shaft'. In the case of Hippolyta's image, the arrow is added by the onlookers: what matters is not the force of a wilful god whose arrow can hit as capriciously as the mistakes of Puck with the magic herb. The moon's arrow is a creation of the lovers and comes from their inner harmony of heart and mind.

The moon is too mysterious for the nature of its order to be easily discernible. There is little place for justice. Titania declares that her quarrel with Oberon has led to 'contagious fogs', floods, rotted corn and the ghastly spectacle of carrion crows gorging themselves on diseased cattle and sheep:

> The fold stands empty in the drownèd field,
> And crows are fatted with the murrion flock;
>
> (II.1.96–97)

As a result, 'no night is now with hymn or carol blest' and the moon punishes this lack of reverence by sending disease:

> Therefore the moon, the governess of floods,
> Pale in her anger, washes all the air,
> That rheumatic diseases do abound
>
> (II.1.103–105)

Such punishment pays little heed to the cause of the offence. In this it harkens back to ancient concepts of the gods, their haughtiness and stern vengefulness. We are for a moment in the world of early classical literature before its later attempts to rationalise primitive belief.

It is characteristic of Shakespeare's comedies that the women are wiser than the men. Certainly this is evident in the two comedies written directly before and after *A Midsummer Night's Dream*. In *Love's Labour's Lost* the Princess of France and her ladies articulate humane values in which the men must be instructed if their suits are to prosper. In *The Merchant of Venice* Portia and Nerissa not only save Antonio from Shylock but eloquently instruct their fiancés in the priorities of love. Titania and Hippolyta are less prominent in *A Midsummer Night's Dream*. Yet before she is put under the influence of the drug, Titania explains why she will not surrender the child to Oberon:

> Set your heart at rest.
> The fairy land buys not the child of me.
> His mother was a votaress of my order,

And in the spicèd Indian air, by night
Full often hath she gossiped by my side,
And sat with me on Neptune's yellow sands
Marking th'embarkèd traders on the flood,
When we have laughed to see the sails conceive
And grow big-bellied with the wanton wind;
Which she with pretty and with swimming gait,
Following — her womb then rich with my young squire —
Would imitate, and sail upon the land
To fetch me trifles, and return again
As from a voyage, rich with merchandise.
But she, being mortal, of that boy did die,
And for her sake do I rear up her boy;
And for her sake I will not part with him.

(II.1.122–137)

This is an enchanting picture of friendship, the 'gossiping' so relaxed, the imitation of the sails by the pregnant girl so robustly joyous. We love Titania for placing loyalty to her dead friend above attraction to Oberon and obedience to him.

Hippolyta corrects Theseus's impatience with the moon in the opening lines and she dissents from his dismissal of the lovers' experiences in the wood:

THESEUS   I never may believe
These antic fables, nor these fairy toys.
Lovers and madmen have such seething brains,
Such shaping fantasies, that apprehend
More than cool reason ever comprehends.
The lunatic, the lover, and the poet
Are of imagination all compact.
One sees more devils than vast hell can hold.
That is the madman. The lover, all as frantic,
Sees Helen's beauty in a brow of Egypt.
The poet's eye, in a fine frenzy rolling,
Doth glance from heaven to earth, from earth to heaven.
And as imagination bodies forth
The forms of things unknown, the poet's pen
Turns them to shapes, and gives to airy nothing
A local habitation and a name.

(V.1.2–17)

Theseus 'never may believe . . . these fairy toys'. He is a muscular rationalist, but also dogmatic and proud. And this extends to a disvaluing of art. What the poet might glimpse of heaven has no appeal to him. Nor will he accept, even as a halfway house, a poet's guessing, intuitive apprehensions into 'things unknown'. The halfway has no interest for him because it is not a journey he wishes to start. He is a resolutely earth-bound empiricist.

Hippolyta is not persuaded by Theseus:

> But all the story of the night told over,
> And all their minds transfigured so together,
> More witnesseth than fancy's images,
> And grows to something of great constancy;
> But howsoever, strange and admirable.
>
> (V.1.23–27)

In debate with her fiancé she stresses the consistency of the transfiguring between the various parties, but the fact that she thinks in terms of transfiguring is what matters to us. For her, great and mysterious changes are possible, impalpable forces may well operate. Pope, some 120 years later, wrote in *The Rape of the Lock*:

> Hear and believe! thy own Importance know,
> Nor bound thy narrow Views to Things below,
> Some secret Truths from Learned Pride conceal'd,
> To Maids alone and Children are reveal'd:
> What tho' no Credit doubting Wits may give?
> The Fair and Innocent shall still believe.
>
> (Canto I, 35–40)

For Pope this sentiment is one of gentle satire his heroine, Belinda, is all too ready to value her own importance. Hippolyta, however, is an authoritative presence. Her opening lines showed an intuitive grasp of the world of the moon and it is fitting that she should now defend it. She herself might one day be a mother and experience, among other of its powers, the mysterious links between the moon and conception with which the play ends.

A Midsummer Night's Dream is a comedy rather than a drama of solemn symbolism, and the comic moments are miraculous in their fusion of robustness with the inner delicacies of the play. Is there a more irrepressible character in Shakespeare than Bottom? His transfiguration is as ludicrous as possible, yet to him it seems a glimpse of heaven:

> When my cue comes, call me, and I will answer. My next is 'Most fair Pyramus'. Heigh ho! Peter Quince! Flute the bellows-mender! Snout the tinker! Starveling! God's my life — stolen hence and left me asleep — I have had a most rare vision. I have had a dream past the wit of man to say what dream it was. Man is but an ass if he go about to expound this dream. Methought I was — there is no man can tell what. Methought I was — and methought I had — but man is but a patched fool if he will offer to say what methought I had. The eye of man hath not heard, the ear of man hath not seen, man's hand is not able to taste, his tongue to conceive, nor his heart to report what my dream was! I will get Peter Quince to write a ballad of this dream. It shall be called 'Bottom's Dream', because it hath no bottom; and I will sing it in the latter end of a play before the Duke.
>
> (IV.1.199–214)

These lines echo the famous description of heaven in 1 Corinthians 2:9.

> Eye hath not seen, nor ear heard, neither have entered into the heart of man, the things which God hath prepared for them that love him.

We laugh at Bottom's exuberant wish to have a 'ballad' and the unselfconsciousness of the pun on his own name, 'because it hath no bottom'. Yet this is a comic way of expressing St Paul's 'hidden wisdom' and the Spirit which 'searcheth all things, yea the deep things of God'. And, in this transfiguring moment, Bottom, even Bottom, gains a stature comparable to that of Theseus who sees no point in the poet's eye glancing 'from earth to heaven'.

There are few more hilarious moments in a good production than Bottom's final entry as Pyramus. But the fun also comes at least in part from the inner strategies the play:

> Sweet moon, I thank thee for thy sunny beams;
> I thank thee, moon, for shining now so bright;
> For by thy gracious, golden, glittering beams

I trust to take of truest Thisbe sight.

(V.1.271–275)

Shakespeare's earlier avoidance of colour is thrown to the winds. The man who found the heavenly in the experience of an ass's head can reach beyond the restrictions of the world of the moon even in pure ludicrousness — just as for Hippolyta the 'silver bow/ New-bent in heaven' marked the beauty of the night which came from accepting its hidden power and workings. Oberon declares that, although a spirit of the night, he loves to sport with the dawn:

> But we are spirits of another sort.
> I with the morning's love have oft made sport,
> And like a forester, the groves may tread
> Even till the eastern gate all fiery red
> Opening on Neptune with fair blessèd beams
> Turns into yellow gold his salt green streams.

(III.2.388–393)

This reaching out and expansiveness informs the world of the play.

AFTERTHOUGHTS

1

Explain the purpose to Gearin-Tosh's argument of the comparison with Chaucer's *The Knight's Tale* on pages 52–54?

2

What significance does this essay suggest for the presence of moonlight in *A Midsummer Night's Dream*?

3

Does your own reading confirm that 'It is characteristic of Shakespeare's comedies that the women are wiser than the men' (page 57)?

4

Could you make a case for arguing that Bottom gains a stature that is not only 'comparable' to that of Theseus (page 60), but is actually superior?

Graham Holderness

Graham Holderness is Head of the Drama Department at Roehampton Institute, and has published numerous works of criticism.

ESSAY

A Midsummer Night's Dream: film and fantasy

THESEUS   I never may believe
These antique fables, nor these fairy toys.
Lovers and madmen have such seething brains,
Such shaping fantasies, that apprehend
More than cool reason ever comprehends.
The lunatic, the lover, and the poet
Are of imagination all compact.
One sees more devils than vast hell can hold.
That is the madman. The lover, all as frantic,
Sees Helen's beauty in a brow of Egypt.
The poet's eye, in a fine frenzy rolling,
Doth glance from heaven to earth, from earth to heaven.
And, as imagination bodies forth
The forms of things unknown, the poet's pen
Turns them to shapes, and gives to airy nothing
A local habitation and a name.

(V.1.2–17)

Theseus's praise of reason falls, of course, at least as far as the audience is concerned, on deaf ears. We have learned from the play to assign more credit, to attach more significance to the realms of 'fantasy' and 'imagination'. The poet's pen has in reality given shape to impossibility and form to the incomprehensible, making us believe, for the duration of a few hours at any rate, in 'such antique fables, and such fairy toys'. When, in the scene for which this speech supplies a prologue, we see the play's courtly lovers, secure in the confident possession of a superior reason, making fun of the vigorous theatrical fantasies of the 'mechanicals', we feel a certain distaste for their mockery, as though at a betrayal.

For Theseus himself, of course, the arbiter of rationality and common sense, these things have no reality and simply defy belief. But the interplay between the action of the drama, and the Duke's exposition of a philosophy of reason, produces a complex exploration of the relations between fact and fantasy, reason and madness, reality and imagination, truth and deception, which is typical of the Renaissance theatre. How would we defend our instinctive belief in what Keats called 'the truth of imagination' against Theseus's persuasive materialism? Perhaps he is right after all, and we ourselves should be included in that company of lunatics, lovers and poets. Yet what is the alternative? Do madness, passion and poetry have no reality, no truth? Is there no substance of reality in the fabric of our dreams?

In this essay I propose to contrast two film versions of *A Midsummer Night's Dream*, in terms of their attempt to deal with the play's ambivalent exploration of fantasy. One is that directed by Max Reinhardt and William Dieterle, made in Hollywood and released in 1935; and the other was directed by Peter Hall, adapted from a Royal Shakespeare Company production, and premiered on American television in 1969.

The lavish, opulent and operatic productions of Max Reinhardt dominated the German theatre in the 1920s, before the radical and innovative productions of the young Marxist writers and directors, such as Brecht and Piscator, began to alter the shape of theatrical culture in the Weimar Republic. Reinhardt was opposed to what he thought of as *literary* forms of drama, particularly naturalism, which in some ways resembled the novel in its realistic characterisation and narrative. Reinhardt thought the production of a play should be a theatre event, a visual, aural and technical action which the audience would experience directly through the senses. Reinhardt also thought that theatre should be 'a meeting-ground for all the arts', a combination of space, light, music, design, acting, mime, dance and the spoken word. In some ways Reinhardt's theatrical conceptions were akin to the 'pure art' of the Aesthetic movement; in other ways they were parallel with Modernism. Unlike the bohemian artists of the 1890s and the great pioneers of Modernism, Reinhardt was however a popular artist; his productions, elaborate and expensive commercial enterprises, toured around the world as packaged samples of the best in German theatrical culture.

Reinhardt's forte was the extravagant, elaborate spectacle, composed by the director acting as a kind of theatrical magician. His stage production of *A Midsummer Night's Dream* was choreographed to Mendelssohn's music, played and danced within elaborate sets. The 'dream' element of the play was conceived and realised as a species of escapist fantasy:

> In Shakespeare's lovely fantasy, I have always seen, above all, a cheering hopeful reminder that since life itself is a dream, we can escape it through our dreams within a dream. When stark reality weighs too heavily upon us, an all-wise providence provides deliverance. Every one has a secret corner into which he can retire and find refuge in Fancy. *A Midsummer Night's Dream* is an invitation to escape reality, a plea for the glorious release to be found in fantasy.[1]

Here the problematical relationship between 'stark reality' and 'dream' is mediated by the intervention of a god-like director, who in the guise of an 'all-wise providence' smooths the reality-burdened spectator into the glorious release of fantasy.

Reinhardt's film version of *A Midsummer Night's Dream* bears many resemblances to the Warner Brothers musicals of the 1930s, and shares with them a common ideology. The specific historical conditions in which both film and spectator were produced (the German Weimar Republic, or the America of the Depression) are projected as an inescapable condition of 'stark reality', which can be transcended or evaded in the pursuit of a

---

[1] Max Reinhardt, Foreword to *A Midsummer Night's Dream* (New York, 1935), p. v.

self-evidently superior fantasy-world of beauty, pleasure and delight. That complex Renaissance sense of the shifting and ambivalent relations between 'reason' and 'fantasy' that we found in Theseus's speech, is here reductively confined to the simplicity of a post-Romantic retreat into the cultivated illusion of 'Fancy'.

Taking Theseus's meditation on imagination as a starting point, *A Midsummer Night's Dream* would appear to be an ideal subject for film adaptation, using exploratory techniques of film narrative and representation to throw the relations between art and artifice, reality and illusion, into a vigorous and liberating visual play. But in Reinhardt's film, Athens is no less of a fantasy than the forest. The civilisation of the city is presented in elaborate visual spectacle as a fantasy landscape, in which minor domestic misunderstandings occur in an atmosphere of romatic comedy:

> The notes of disharmony sounded pose no real threat in the overall atmosphere of triumph and celebration.[2]

The critic Jack Jorgen's musical metaphor ('notes of disharmony') calls attention to the operatic quality of this film, its dramatic incident and visual narrative choreographed to a musical score. Jorgens goes further, proposing that the film can be regarded as a kind of 'tone-poem', which has actually shaped its visual representations in musical terms:

> The total graphic feeling is like a flow of bright palace crescendos, dusky forest cadenzas, pizzicato glimpses of glistening dewdrops, and largo passages of mysterious and lovely moonlit creatures — the whole thoroughly and ornamentally orchestrated for the eye.[3]

Here the film is being interpreted as a kind of Wagnerian music-drama; and it is true that Reinhardt's stage practice often seemed to aspire to the totally integrated aesthetic completeness of a perfect work of art. Jorgens on the other hand argues that the film is more complex than Reinhardt's own description of it

---

[2] Jack Jorgens, *Shakespeare on Film* (Bloomington, Indiana, 1977), p. 40.
[3] Ibid.

as a playful recreation of Shakespeare's 'lovely fantasy'; there are certain elements in it which foreshadow the 'darker dreams' of Peter Brook and Peter Hall. Any oppositional or contradictory elements within the play are however firmly integrated into a cohesive totality analogous to the harmony of music;

> The discord becomes musical ... All of this repetition and coun-terpoint is, of course, reinforced by Mendelssohn's music, in which themes and styles associated with the plot ... are subtly varied and blended in a harmonious whole.[4]

Shakespeare's play, as Theseus's speech on reason alone will sufficiently indicate, depends for its significant structure on the establishing of contradictions. If there is no sense of *difference* between city and forest, court and carpenter's shop, between the Dionysiac irrationality of emotion and fantasy, and the Apollo-nian rigidity of intellect and law, then the play's contents will flow and blend into a monotonous neutrality — either Theseus's dimension of 'cool reason', or the alternative realm of 'antique fable'. It is up to the director (as it is up to the critical reader) how to interpret the structure of these contradictions: the play can with equal legitimacy be seen as a resolution of discords, or as an interweaving of contraries which are left precariously balanced and essentially unresolved in the conclusion. If the drama is produced as pure fantasy, with no sense of difference, then clearly the interpretation will automatically commit itself to the first of these possibilities. In Reinhardt's version of *A Midsummer Night's Dream*, the seamless unity of a perfected work of art transcends the irreducible complexities of 'stark reality', and offers the spectator nothing more intriguing than a transient and compensatory wish-fulfilment fantasy. As we shall see presently, Reinhardt's remarkable handling of the film's conclusion offers some degree of qualification to this general judgement.

Reinhardt's film was aimed at the commercial cinema, and at the mass audience of the 1930s which enjoyed musicals, romantic comedy and farce. Peter Hall's version belongs to a very different cultural context, that of a Royal Shakespeare

---

[4] Ibid., p. 48.

Company production initially turned into a film for American television. Hall's conception of how to film a Shakespeare play was expounded in a 1969 interview with Roger Manvell:

> The greatest influence on me, on my generation, was Leavis, who believed above everything in a critical examination of the text, the search for meaning and metaphor . . . The traditional Shakespeare film in English has ignored any kind of reflection of the aural pattern in the visual pattern. They should surely match. In the *Dream* my aim was to create a picture rhythm by cutting to the verbal pattern — that is, on the caesura, or at the end of the line.
>
> Too much normal film art contradicts the techniques of the plays, at least as far as their most important element, the text, is concerned. But the medium of film can certainly be used to communicate the text most effectively, even to the extent of making its meaning clearer than is sometimes possible in the theatre . . .
>
> This is not a film *from* a stage production or a film *based* on the play. It attempts to bend the medium of film to reveal the full quality of the text.[5]

Where Reinhardt openly translated Shakespeare's play into a contemporary medium of popular culture, subordinating the dramatic text to spectacle and music, Hall insisted that the film should be a visual embodiment of the text, fleshing the verbal structure with the concrete experience it signifies, but controlled absolutely by the authoritative structure and rhythm of the text. Hall's approach to film was therefore much more *literary* then Reinhardt's. Reinhardt strove to escape from a literary kind of theatre altogether: Hall wanted to collapse the medium of film back into the text. He even wondered whether perhaps his film of *A Midsummer Night's Dream* was 'not a film at all', but an experiment in forcing the values privileged by that particular (Leavisite) school of literary criticism — muscular verse, concrete imagery, the authentic rhythm of the speaking voice, integrated organic form — into the medium of film.

---

[5] Quoted in Roger Manvell, *Shakespeare and the Film* (South Brunswick and New York, 1979), pp. 121–126.

Hall's film opens with a deliberate disruption of naturalist film conventions: superimposed on the image of a typical neo-classical 'English country house', surrounded by visual associations of order and authority, appears the title 'Athens'. In place of the more familiar naturalistic techniques of cinema, which would require here an 'establishing shot' to give the spectator a clear idea of 'where' and 'when' we are, this film subverts normal habits of perception by showing us a stereotypical image, and then attaching to it a surprisingly discordant label. The 'Athenian' court is set in a chaste, barren and colourless environment, filmed with a telephoto lens to make the screen image less solid, more two-dimensional.

To take the spectator from court to forest, Hall uses further disruptive devices such as 'jump-cuts', letting the narrative rhythm of the text produce a cinematic technique of *montage*. The forest sequences were shot with a hand-held camera, so the spectator is aware, from the slightly irregular movements of the frame, of the camera as a recorder of this simulated 'reality'. The actors frequently address the camera directly, demolishing the 'fourth wall' convention of naturalism. The magic of Oberon is emulated by conjuring tricks of cinematography, as Puck appears and disappears, and the disjunctive editing confuses all regular sense of time and space. Puck's concluding invitation to the audience to:

> Think but this, and all is mended:
> That you have but slumbered here
> While these visions did appear.
> And this weak and idle theme,
> No more yielding but a dream.

(V.1.414–418)

is spoken in darkness. Puck snaps his fingers, and it is morning. Which is the reality, which the illusion: daylight and the solid façade of Theseus's rationalistic Athens, or the 'magic' of the forest, as rendered by the film's playful and defamiliarising cinematography?

In many ways Hall's version of *A Midsummer Night's Dream* produces from a filmic imitation of the text an experimental, avant-garde form of cinema which is highly successful in representing the play's ambivalent exploration of the shifting, elusive relations between reality and illusion. It is precisely because literature and film are such different forms of narrative and representation, that the attempt to make one imitate the other precisely resulted in a radically new method of screening Shakespeare.

Hall also, however, followed Leavis's critical method in his general interpretation of the play's closure, and in this respect the film works to close up, in a move towards ideological reconciliation, what its avant-garde cinematography has opened. From Leavis, Hall learned that a successful work of art is one in which inner contradictions are perfectly balanced and reconciled, in a formal structure which mirrors the moral stability of the author. When Hall's 'mechanicals' present their play, the courtly audience is thoroughly involved in a shared experience of festive celebration. Hall cheated on his respect for the text by cutting some of the courtiers' condescending comments, and dramatised a scene in which the lovers seem to have benefited from their flirtation with the occult, and can take their places in a society united into community by the combined magic of supernatural agency and enthusiastic popular theatricals.

In this respect Hall's film provides a curious contrast with Reinhardt's. When Reinhardt's 'mechanicals' return to perform their burgomask dance to the Athenian court, they find the courtiers gone, having forgotten all about them, and leaving the amateur actors playing to an empty house. This detail may be little more than a director's nightmare: but it is enough to cast a shadow, very much in the spirit of Shakespearean comedy, across the play's harmonious resolution. So Reinhardt's operatic extravaganza is shadowed by the foregrounding of an unassimilated element, excluded from the strategic alliance of court and forest; while Peter Hall's self-reflexive and radical cinematic experiment is ultimately pulled back towards a resolution expressing a faith in the possibility of community and reconciliation which would be hard to find in Shakespeare's ambivalent dramatic text.

AFTERTHOUGHTS

1

Do you agree that an audience feels 'a certain distaste' for the courtiers' mockery of the performance of *Pyramus and Thisbe*?

2

What general criticism does Holderness make of Max Reinhardt's film of *A Midsummer Night's Dream* (pages 64–67)? What does he believe was lost?

3

Explain what Holderness means by suggesting that Hall's approach to filming the play was 'much more *literary*' (page 68) that Reinhardt's.

4

Which of the two film endings, as described by Holderness (page 70), seems to you preferable?

Michael Mangan

*Michael Mangan lectures in English at
Sheffield University, and is the author of
numerous critical studies.*

ESSAY

'The tedious brief death of young Pyramus': illusions and the breaking of illusion in *A Midsummer Night's Dream*

]

A stage death can make an audience cry in sympathy or can
move it to tears of laughter. To watch somebody enact death,
pretend to die, is a strange kind of experience. If it is done
effectively it can be harrowing — presenting every member of
the audience with an intimation of their own mortality. Con-
versely, a stage death done badly is ridiculous: a moment
designed to excite pathos ends up producing giggles. It might be
due to bad acting, or bad writing, or both. It may come about
simply because the conventions by which a stage death is
heralded seem to an audience to be clumsy and outdated. Lines
like 'Villain, thou hast killed me', or 'Thus die I' trigger laughter
all too easily — as do long and extravagant poetical speeches
from the mouth of a dying character. To put it at its most
general, a stage death fails to work because a spell has been

broken: the spell which allows the audience to participate imaginatively in the 'reality' (not necessarily an illusionistic one) of the stage experience. The moment when an audience giggles inappropriately signals the breakdown of the creative partnership between stage and audience.

Pyramus's death in '*A tedious brief scene of young Pyramus/ And his love Thisbe*' is a glorious failure. Here, Shakespeare parodies the stage convention of the dying speech — a convention of which he himself made plentiful use elsewhere in his career. In *A Midsummer Night's Dream*, however, he sends it up unmercifully. Pyramus stabs himself and declaims:

> Thus die I — thus, thus, thus.
> Now am I dead,
> Now am I fled;
> My soul is in the sky.
> Tongue, lose thy light;
> Moon, take thy flight;
> Now die, die, die, die, die.
>
> (V.1.292–298)

The basic joke of this dying-speech parody (at the risk of labouring the obvious) is not merely the incongruity of someone continuing to talk after a mortal wound; it is the way in which, on the stage, language staves off death. The character is 'dead', but will not lie down until his language ceases. In this case, Shakespeare couples with this the joke against the ham actor who makes as much as he can of his final moments — making a 'good' death by wringing the greatest possible amount of spectacle out of the event. It is a paradox that the harder the actor tries to squeeze emotion out of the moment, the more likely he is to defeat his own purpose. Thus the audience, moved at first perhaps to sympathise with the character's death, is confronted continually with the actor's prolongation of the dying moment, so that sympathy turns to laughter.

Pyramus's speech (as no one has ever failed to grasp) is a remorseless parody of this. It is written so as to present a comic actor with a god-given opportunity to repeat the joke almost obsessively. 'Thus die I,' says Pyramus. From that moment on, until the end of that short speech, there are thirteen (thirteen!) opportunities for the actor to 'die' on stage and then come back to life to add another 'thus', or another 'die' or another phrase about the soul, the tongue or the moon. At its most basic it is a matter of an actor saying 'I'm dead — No, I'm not — Yes, I am — No, I'm not.' It is the childhood game of peekaboo, where the parent vanishes and returns before the child's eyes. As the audience 'accepts' the death of the character, the actor returns to play the game over again. The audience is left in a continual state of comic flux, uncertain as to whether the fictional death has actually taken place or not. The comedy arises because attention is directed, not towards the illusion of someone dying, but towards the gap between that intended illusion and the reality of Nick Bottom's terrible acting.

2

It is a commonplace of criticism of *A Midsummer Night's Dream* that it is a play which is concerned with matters of illusion and reality. Most importantly, Shakespeare uses the play's concentration on this issue to explore the nature of the theatrical experience itself. In *A Midsummer Night's Dream* the magic of the wood outside Athens and the magic of theatrical creation are constantly being compared to each other; the ability of art and magic to transform reality and to create new realities is one of the central obsessions of the play. Nowhere is this more clearly shown than in the famous speech of Theseus in Act V scene 1, where the very notion of the writer's creativity is seen as suspect:

> HIPPOLYTA 'Tis strange, my Theseus, that these lovers speak of.
> THESEUS More strange than true. I never may believe
> These antique fables, nor these fairy toys.
> Lovers and madmen have such seething brains,
> Such shaping fantasies, that apprehend
> More than cool reason ever comprehends.
> The lunatic, the lover, and the poet
> Are of imagination all compact.
> One sees more devils than vast hell can hold.
> That is the madman. The lover, all as frantic,
> Sees Helen's beauty in a brow of Egypt.

The poet's eye, in a fine frenzy rolling,
Doth glance from heaven to earth, from earth to heaven.
And as imagination bodies forth
The forms of things unknown, the poet's pen
Turns them to shapes, and gives to airy nothing
A local habitation and a name.
Such tricks hath strong imagination
That if it would but apprehend some joy,
It comprehends some bringer of that joy.
Or in the night, imagining some fear,
How easy is a bush supposed a bear?

(V.1.1–22)

Theseus's speech here is a pivotal point: it refers back to the world of the wood, and simultaneously points forward to the mechanicals' performance of *Pyramus and Thisbe*. His instant linking of 'Lovers and madmen' performs syntactically what Shakespeare enacted structurally in setting the action of the middle part of the play in the wood outside Athens. If Athens, with Theseus as its duke, is the world of philosophy, logic and reason, what lies outside the city boundaries is 'wood'. The Middle English meaning of that word reverberates through the play: in the English of Shakespeare's forebears the word 'wood' was an adjective, meaning 'mad'. The availability of this old meaning of the word to Shakespeare's own generation is made clear by Demetrius in Act II scene 1: 'And here am I, and wood within this wood/ Because I cannot meet my Hermia' (lines 192–193). And outside Athens, the city of reason, lies the wood of madness, where magic and impossibilities hold sway.

So Theseus, here portrayed as a thoroughgoing rationalist, touches off with his words associations which go far beyond his own comprehension. He sees his task as being to apply cool reason to the situation — to reduce all he sees to the most prosaic of rationalisations. Yet in all sorts of ways, even as he speaks, his position is undercut. Firstly, of course, there is the basic joke that Theseus, himself the creation of a 'poet's pen', is here denigrating the very creative act that gave him breath to speak. The irony is compounded by the fact that the character whom Shakespeare chooses to represent Athenian logic is not Plato, Socrates or Aristotle — not, that is, one of the philosophers of ancient history — but Theseus, a creature himself of myth and legend. Theseus's dubious status is further emphasised when, as is often the case on the stage, the parts of Oberon and Theseus are doubled (as are those of Hippolyta and Titania). But even without this, the ironic undercutting of his speech is clear enough, for we, the audience, *know* that he is wrong. We have seen Acts II, III and IV of the play, and we know that whatever account the lovers gave of it, the 'truth' is more outlandish than Theseus's well-ordered world can conceive of. In Theseus's limited world-view there is room only for the truth of everyday, common-sense experience: all that lies beyond that is 'antique fable'. That which is 'strange' is almost certainly not also 'true'. We know better.

Hippolyta is more open-minded than Theseus, and if her reply that the lovers' account, 'More witnesseth than fancy's images' (V.1.25) is tentative and unlikely to sway Theseus, it shows at least that she herself is not convinced by his 'cool reason'. But as the lovers enter, the attention turns from one kind of extension and expansion of reality to another. The interest in the wood as a place of separate realities is displaced onto the stage itself. What is now introduced is the question of the entertainments at the court of Duke Theseus to celebrate the wedding — not just of himself and Hippolyta, now, but also of Lysander and Hermia, and Demetrius and Helena. At this point the play becomes hugely self-reflexive.

3

Exactly how self-reflexive is difficult to say. 'Most scholars are agreed', says *Arden* editor Harold F. Brooks, 'that the *Dream* was designed to grace a wedding in a noble household.' We should be a little careful about this kind of information. It is always tempting to try to re-create imaginatively the original performance conditions of a Shakespeare play — as if by doing so we could conjure up the 'true' version of it. But the information is uncertain. Nobody has proved irrefutably that the play *was* written and performed as a wedding piece; indeed nobody is even sure whose wedding it was supposed to be written for, although the front-runners are Thomas Heneage and Mary, Countess of Southampton, and Elizabeth Carey and Thomas, son of Henry Lord Berkeley. Moreover, even if it *could* be proved beyond a shadow of a doubt that the play had been written for a particular occasion, we would still have to ask how important such information was. For plays, unlike novels, poems or paintings, are not static objects but fluid works of art subject to continual restaging, reinterpretation and re-creation. This is true from one age to another, of course, but it is equally true of the play as it existed in Shakespeare's own time. To put it bluntly, the play may well have been originally written for a wedding in an aristocratic household, but it was also regularly played on the London stage before the general populace. When the first Quarto appeared in the booksellers' shops in 1600, it was advertised on its title page as having 'been sundry times publickely acted, by the Right honourable, the Lord Chamberlaine his servants'. We may well conclude that whatever the genesis of the play, the reason we still read it, watch it and perform it today is that it transcends its origins — that it works over and above the context of any specific occasion it might have been written for.

Nonetheless, the conjecture that *A Midsummer Night's Dream* was originally written for a specific occasion deserves some entertaining. To know — or even to be able to make a plausible guess — about the original conditions of creation of a work of art may enable us to understand more clearly why it is the way it is. And if it is the case that the *Dream* was originally written as a play for private performance at a marriage celebration, then Act V of the play effectively turns into drama the very circumstances of the play's own staging. In this 'noble household' a play is being staged to celebrate a wedding. In this play we see — a noble household in which a play is about to be staged to celebrate a wedding . . . In *Hamlet*, Shakespeare talks about the function of drama as being 'to hold a mirror up to nature'. In *A Midsummer Night's Dream*, the mirror which the dramatist holds up is a multifaceted fairground mirror, full of planes and curves, a mirror whose job is not merely to reflect a single truth but one which distorts everyday reality in such a way as to throw new, and often strange, light upon it.

In Acts II to IV the audience has been presented with a series of tinkerings with notions of reality and unreality. The movement consists of a continual series of shifts between the unfamiliar and the familiar. The audience starts to watch a play: the world of that play is the alien one of ancient Greece. Yet ancient Greece is then brought back to the familiar level by the portrayal of the 'mechanicals' — familiar Elizabethan social stereotypes and very 'English'. Then there is the 'wood' outside Athens. A step further away from everyday reality into one where supernatural powers rule and fairies play tricks on humans. Yet here too the familiar is reinstated; the supernatural catastrophes the fairies bring about are located in the world of the English Tudor countryside where the 'nine men's morris is filled up with mud', where the familiar English sprite Robin Goodfellow (Puck) wanders amongst English woodland flora. So the scenes within the wood do two things simultaneously: they take the audience progressively further and further away from its own customary everyday reality, into a world which is governed by magic and wonder; but they also reinstate a sense of home, a sense of Englishness.

Now, in Act V a similar kind of trick is to be played with ideas of reality. In one sense the mechanicals' presentation of *Pyramus and Thisbe* will be one stage further removed from reality — a play within a play, of course. Yet it will also confront the real-life audience with an image of itself and, in the case of the conjectural aristocrats at the wedding feast, a very direct image indeed! There is an edgy kind of humour here, for if the dramatist satirises the inadequacies of his own art-form in the incompetent playing of the mechanicals, he also presents a not very flattering image of an audience.

Let us look at these two points in order. Firstly, the mechanicals' play is an obvious butt of humour. Shakespeare does everything in his power to make sure that the 'tedious brief scene' cannot possibly have the tragic effect that its actors intend. The players are inept, the direction incompetent; the conventions are outmoded, the verse generally lame and at times execrable:

>   But stay — O spite!
>   But mark, poor Knight,
>   What dreadful dole is here?
>   Eyes, do you see? —
>   How can it be?

O dainty duck! O dear!
Thy mantle good —
What stained with blood!
Approach, ye Furies fell.
O Fates, come, come,
Cut thread and thrum,
Quail, crush, conclude, and quell.

(V.1.268–279)

The mechanicals are ridiculous in their anxiety that the whole thing might actually appear too realistic and 'frighten the ladies'. Because of this they repeatedly dismantle whatever illusion *might* be available to an audience: '"Deceiving me" is Thisbe's cue,' explains Bottom (V.1.181–182); 'Then know that I as Snug the joiner am/ A lion fell,' explains the joiner (lines 219–220); 'This lanthorn doth the hornèd moon present' (line 233) — and best of all, Snout's introduction, 'In this same interlude it doth befall/ That I — one Snout by name — present a wall' (lines 153–154). The performance of *Pyramus and Thisbe* thus consists of one shattering of dramatic illusion after another. But the point is that there is more to the performance than merely parody. That is there, certainly, and it would be a foolish production that omitted it; but what happens in the play-within-the-play goes beyond a simple send-up of naïve drama. One of the things which carries Act V beyond mere parody is the way in which Shakespeare uses the presence of the onstage aristocratic audience.

There are two ways of looking at the continual interruptions of the courtiers into the performance of *Pyramus and Thisbe*. One is, simply laugh along with them: to side with them and to enjoy poking fun at these incompetent amateurs, these common workmen who attempt so unskilfully to put on a classical tragedy. On the other hand, however, we might well find the courtiers' comments and interjections rather a nuisance. The class politics of the situation may make us feel a little uncomfortable, and we may feel that the witty, sophisticated jests of the privileged at the expense of the artisan classes wear thin rather quickly. In any case, do we really *need* their commentary in order to appreciate that the mechanicals are poor actors? Isn't the spirit of their remarks rather mean-minded, in fact?

We may be particularly inclined to take this view of the

courtiers considering the short exchange that takes place between Hippolyta and Theseus immediately prior to the performance itself. The entertainment having been decided, Hippolyta expresses doubts about their own courtesy in choosing such an ill-fitted group:

> THESEUS   I will hear that play,
> For never anything can be amiss
> When simpleness and duty tender it.
>
> . . .
>
> HIPPOLYTA   I love not to see wretchedness o'ercharged,
> And duty in his service perishing . . .
>
> . . .
>
> He says they can do nothing in this kind.
> THESEUS   The kinder we, to give them thanks for nothing.
> Our sport shall be to take what they mistake;
> And what poor duty cannot do, noble respect
> Takes it in might, not merit.

(V.1.81–92)

Hippolyta's scruples, Theseus's response, seem gentle and courteous. Theseus in particular appears civilised and rather gracious at this moment. He is extending the phenomenological rationalism of his earlier bush-and-bear speech (which put much of the duty of interpretation upon the observer) into the area of aesthetic theory. His insight is that the work of art exists in the communication between the speaker and the listener, and his project is to establish the court as a sympathetic audience which cooperates with the artists (taking more of their fair share than is usual in this sort of partnership, to be sure) in the dynamic of creating a fictional reality. In that, however, the fine words of his theory are in marked contrast to the practice that we see once the play actually starts. The tones in which the Duke and his young hangers-on (only in name, I think, are they the young lovers with whom we might have sympathised in the earlier acts of the play) interrupt the action of the mechanicals' play have little to do with 'noble respect'. They palpably fail to live up to the image of the generous audience which Theseus proposes.

In this way Shakespeare confronts the audience with two alternative possible reactions, neither of which is completely satisfactory in itself. Simply to laugh at the mechanicals is to align oneself uncomfortably with the sneering courtiers. Yet *not* to laugh, and to concentrate on censuring the courtiers for their lack of generosity, is to ignore just how well *Pyramus and Thisbe* works as a parody of drama: it is very funny on stage. For an audience, in fact, the essential experience of *A Midsummer Night's Dream* is that of being repeatedly suspended between two conflicting realities: the 'wood' and the 'city', the healing energies of the fairy kingdom and their anarchic destructiveness, belief in illusion and awareness of its essential falsity . . . Which brings us back to Pyramus and his death-scene.

4

Bottom/Pyramus, we noted at the beginning of this essay, continually puts off the moment of death. And just as he seems to die and then repeatedly revives for one more line, word or phrase, so the play as a whole frequently teases the audience with the possibility of an ending, only to come back to life again. The process started at the end of Act IV, where the lovers' story seemed all but over. As they and Theseus left the stage, returning to Athens and their happy ending, the play itself might have suitably ended — were it not for the fact that Nick Bottom, asleep in a corner of the stage, suddenly wakes up and lets us know that there's more to come. Act V runs its course with the mechanicals' play, and once Pyramus has died and the play-within-the-play is done, that again could well be an appropriate ending to *A Midsummer Night's Dream*. And indeed, the play appears to wrap itself up at that point: 'Will it please you to see the epilogue, or to hear a Bergomask dance between two of our company?' asks Bottom (V.1.343–345). Theseus chooses the Bergomask — and the play is ended by a dance. Since this was common practice in the Elizabethan playhouse, it looks very much as if this dance is to signal the end not only of *Pyramus and Thisbe* but also of *A Midsummer Night's Dream*. It would have been a neat and fitting conclusion. But the dance ends and the play continues. Theseus steps forward and delivers an effective epilogue which clears the stage of all the actors:

> The iron tongue of midnight hath told twelve.
> Lovers, to bed; 'tis almost fairy time.
>
> . . .
>
> > Sweet friends, to bed.
> A fortnight hold we this solemnity
> In nightly revels and new jollity.
>
> > > > (V.1.353–354, 358–360)

The audience is getting ready to clap by now — but the clearing of the stage is not quite complete: as the mortal characters make their exit, Puck steps forward to deliver *his* epilogue:

> Now the hungry lion roars
> > And the wolf behowls the moon
> . . .
> And we fairies, that do run
> > By the triple Hecate's team
> From the presence of the sun
> > Following darkness like a dream,
> Now are frolic. Not a mouse
> Shall disturb this hallowed house.
> I am sent with broom before
> To sweep the dust behind the door.
>
> > > > (V.1.361–362, 373–380)

This should be an even more definite cue for the action to end, as Puck's last couplet begins to question his own status: is he supernatural being or actor-cum-stage-hand? The epilogue's traditional task of modulating from the world of the fiction back to the world of the audience's everyday reality seems to have been accomplished. But again Shakespeare is only teasing the audience. Oberon and Titania return to the stage for their final number. A speech, then a song and dance. Once more the play seems to have ended. Oberon's final blessing of the marriage beds might be part of that song and dance, or all or part of it may be said after the dance has finished; if the latter there is another false ending. The technique, by now, is beginning to resemble the ending of a Rossini overture: the melody comes to a fortissimo climax, the audience is ready to applaud, then realises it is not quite over: there is one more chord to come ('Do we clap now?') — then another ('Now?') — then yet another, and one more. It is disorienting.

But after Oberon's blessing the stage empties again. Surely, this must be the end? No, once again, Puck frustrates the potential moment of closure. He stays — or returns — for one final address to the audience, modulating more completely now into the actor who asks for applause rather than the 'serpent's tongue' of the audience's hisses. Even in this speech Shakespeare cannot resist one last twitch of the rope: 'So goodnight unto you all,' says Puck — but stays yet another moment for his punch line:

> Give me your hands if we be friends,
> And Robin shall restore amends.

(V.1.427–428)

Now, finally, the play really is over. Like Nick Bottom's Pyramus, it has staved off its own death several times, but finally it relaxes its grip on the spectators and allows them to applaud if they will, and then to leave the theatre, to go back to their homes, their lives. Yet this series of false endings, the continual uncertainty as to whether the play is actually over yet, have put the audience into a position at the end of the play which is rather like that of the lovers in Act IV scene 2 — unsure which world they inhabit, that of fantasy or of reality, but faced with the claims of both:

> DEMETRIUS   Are you sure
> That we are awake? It seems to me
> That yet we sleep, we dream. Do you not think
> The Duke was here, and bid us follow him?
> HERMIA   Yea, and my father.
> HELENA   And Hippolyta.
> LYSANDER   And he did bid us follow to the temple.
> DEMETRIUS   Why, then, we are awake: let's follow him,
> And by the way let's recount our dreams.

(IV.1.191–198)

AFTERTHOUGHTS

1

To what extent, in your view, does *A Midsummer Night's Dream* offer an exploration of 'the nature of theatrical experience itself' (page 74)?

2

What arguments can you see for having actors 'double' the parts of Oberon/Theseus and Hipployta/Titania (page 76)?

3

What do you understand by 'self-reflexive' (page 76)?

4

What links does Mangan note between the construction of Bottom's final speech as Pyramus and the ending of *A Midsummer Night's Dream* itself (pages 81–83)? Do you agree with his interpretation of the effect that this has on an audience?

Diana Devlin

Diana Devlin has taught Theatre Arts and directed extensively in colleges and universities in Great Britain and the USA. She is a director of the Shakespeare Globe Project, and now works at Leeds Castle in Kent.

ESSAY

'Sweet Bully Bottom': an assessment of Bottom's role in *A Midsummer Night's Dream*

Three worlds converge in *A Midsummer Night's Dream*: the world of the lovers, the world of the fairies, and the world of the workmen. In performance, the relative dominance of each group depends on the quality of the acting. In some productions, Oberon, Titania and Puck take the lead, the lovers seem pale and insignificant beside them, and the workmen merely provide comic relief. In other productions, the mortals take focus, and the fairy world is simply the dramatic environment in which their actions are played out. The character of Bottom is especially open to various emphases. He is the clown of the play, and Shakespeare knew that the clown, of all actors, is capable of making his performance take more and more of the audience's attention, of actually 'stealing the show'. In *Hamlet*, the clowns are specifically instructed to speak 'no more than is set down for them', and not to distract the audience's attention when 'some necessary question of the play be then to be considered', (*Hamlet*,

III.2.38, 41–42). However, some of the clown characters that Shakespeare drew do undoubtedly contribute more than comic relief to the drama; the tradition of the sad clown is a long one, and Shakespeare's Falstaff in *Henry IV, Part 1* and *Part 2*, Feste in *Twelfth Night*, and the Fool in *King Lear* are examples. The role of Bottom, too, I believe, offers the clown-actor the possibility of creating a comic performance which does more than rouse laughter as the butt of Puck's practical joke, and as the object of ridicule at court.

Nick Bottom plays a small and involuntary part in the plot of the play, but it has significance. He is the creature Titania first sees when she awakens with the magic juice on her eyes which makes her love him obsessively. Because of her obsession, Oberon is able to win from her the Indian boy who is the main cause of the quarrel between them, and their lovers' tiff is resolved. This resolution has wider implications, because, as King and Queen of the fairy world, they have power over nature. While they are in disharmony, we learn, the seasons have been turned topsy-turvy, and the natural yearly cycle disrupted. So Bottom is like the hero of a Holy Grail romance, achieving the restoration of peace and fruitfulness in the land. Except that he does it quite unknowingly, and without actually 'doing' anything, just as when he is playing the part of Pyramus, his script has been prepared, this time by Puck. And Puck, as a comic playwright, makes the whole episode ridiculous and absurd by placing an ass's head on Bottom, hoping that the timing will work out so that Titania falls in love with Bottom-as-ass.

In the original production, the part of Bottom was probably played by the clown Will Kemp. From his very first entrance, the audience was already predisposed to laugh at him, and Shakespeare gave Kemp many comic opportunities. First, the clown asks if he is to play 'a lover or a tyrant'. Then he goes on to imitate an outmoded style of theatre:

> The raging rocks
> And shivering shocks
> Shall break the locks
>   Of prison gates,
> And Phibbus' car
> Shall shine from far

And make and mar
The foolish Fates.

(I.2.27–34)

Later, he parodies the custom of men playing women's parts, even though the play as a whole makes great demands on that art, as boys and young men undertook the female romantic roles of Hippolyta, Hermia, Helena and Titania. He also pre-empts the joke of Snug-as-Lion by himself offering that he will 'roar you as gently as any sucking dove. I will roar you an 'twere any nightingale' (I.2.77–78).

One of the characteristics of a clown, which Will Kemp must have had, is that he remains incontrovertibly and unrepentantly himself, like Frankie Howerd or Rowan Atkinson today. Shakespeare builds the comedy on that very fact. In the second rehearsal scene, Bottom suggests a prologue which will assure the audience 'that I, Pyramus, am not Pyramus, but Bottom the weaver' (III.1.19–20). This line should get a laugh because it is so obvious that he is Bottom. 'This will put them out of their fear': a second laugh at the impossibility of being frightened by a clown.

As this second rehearsal scene progresses, Shakespeare builds up the endearing qualities of Bottom's character which will impinge on his later development. Unlike the later comic character of Falstaff, Bottom has no arrogance. His desire to play all the parts is not conceit but enthusiasm, and that is easily channelled into the questions of stagecraft that have to be addressed. He is quick to suggest solutions to such problems as creating moonlight and a crannied wall; and although the fusspot Peter Quince is often outmatched by Bottom's inventive energy, there is no suggestion of a power struggle between them. After speaking his first lines, Bottom obediently disappears into the bushes, where Puck manages to get the ass's head on him.

After the comic horrified reaction to Bottom's transformation, he is left alone with only the audience, the sleeping Titania, and perhaps a lone sentinel who is still guarding her. He believes his friends are trying to frighten him, but he is determined to stand his ground, and even to sing 'that they shall hear I am not afraid' (III.1.117). He remains, he sings, and Titania awakes. Thus, his unflappability and his strong sense of his own identity help bring about Oberon's wishes.

How should we regard the role of Bottom-as-ass? From Oberon's point of view, his wish has seemingly been granted, for he has hoped that Titania will fall in love with a beast: 'Be it on lion, bear, or wolf, or bull' (II.1.180), and later, 'Be it ounce or cat or bear,/ Pard, or boar with bristled hair' (II.2.36–37). Bestial transformation is usually horrific; but not perhaps in this case. Just as the lion in *Pyramus and Thisbe* will be less than fearsome because it is only Snug the joiner, so the ass that Titania couples with has no power to appal or terrify, because it is really only Bottom.

Though translated, Bottom remains consistent to the clown character he already was. The ass's head changes him very little, because, of all Shakespeare's characters, he resembles nothing so much as a loveable ass, even before Puck gets to him. For some actors, playing two scenes with an ass's head covering your face would be a distinct disadvantage. But a mask can also help an actor, giving extra emphasis to gestures and body language. A good actor playing Bottom uses the head-mask as powerful additional means of comic expression, turning his head to catch the best postures, using its length and long ears to reinforce the absurdity that this is, and is not, Bottom. Unlike the other characters under enchantment, he is unchanged by the spell. He converses serenely with Titania and her fairies, adopting a straightforward and courteous manner which will also stand him in good stead at Theseus's court. He even comes up with a nugget of homely wisdom that has some bearing on the whole play: 'And yet, to say the truth, reason and love keep little company together nowadays — the more the pity that some honest neighbours will not make them friends' (III.1.136–138). This, perhaps, is the first indication that we might learn by seeing the world from his point of view.

In the second scene of his transformation, we are able to consider more deeply what is happening both to Titania and to Bottom. He has begun to acquire some of the attributes of a real donkey, requiring to have his head scratched, and to munch on some 'good dry oats'. Puck, or the forest, has apparently effected real magic, not just a theatrical change of appearance. The actor will probably explore ways of modifying his voice to resemble the characteristic braying of an ass. But he still remains Bottom, jovially suggesting some music on the tong and bones, and generally behaving like a jolly uncle who's being given a birthday party.

Titania continues to be in thrall to her new-found passion. Helena had prepared the audience for such a phenomenon when she mused on the nature of love:

> Things base and vile, holding no quantity,
> Love can transpose to form and dignity.

(I.1.232–233)

With the help of the magic flower, this has been done. Puck has proudly told Oberon, 'My mistress with a monster is in love' (III.2.6). Describing Bottom as 'The shallowest thickskin of that barren sort', he draws attention to the double incongruity of Titania's fixation; even without the ass's head, this would be a grotesque mismatch.

Although there is a dark side to Titania's love, it is important to remember that throughout the scene, Bottom is impervious to her blandishments. If he responded, then sexuality of the grossest kind would dominate the scene. As it is, the clownishness of Bottom ensures that comedy is to the fore, and that the grotesque undercurrent is kept well below the surface. Its presence is mainly felt by jealous Oberon, who talks of Bottom as 'this hateful fool' (IV.1.48) and determines to undo 'This hateful imperfection of her eyes' (IV.1.62). Yet the language used to describe Titania's love while she is actually embracing Bottom is neither comic nor grotesque, but voluptuous and sensual. She compares herself to an entangling plant:

> So doth the woodbine the sweet honeysuckle
> Gently entwist; the female ivy so
> Enrings the barky fingers of the elm.

(IV.1.41–44)

And Oberon describes meeting her when:

> . . . she his hairy temples then had rounded
> With coronet of fresh and fragrant flowers.   (IV.1.50–51)

At these moments, we see Titania's power over the innocent Bottom. The artist Marc Chagall captured this innocence in a painting of Titania caressing a pretty, white, sad-faced ass.

Thus, the horrific, the alluring and the comic are all combined in the effect created by the Fairy Queen's dotage on Bottom; and he is seen from multiple points of view as a fool, a beast and an innocent.

We come now to the moments of awakening, when all the characters who have been under enchantment wake up to a changed reality. Titania is the first, fulfilling all that Oberon could have hoped, with her waking words: 'My Oberon'. She remembers her 'dream' at once: 'Methought I was enamoured of an ass', and straight away rejects him, 'O, how mine eyes do loath his visage now!' (IV.1.75–78). Bottom's part in the central plot is finished. Puck removes his head. Oberon leads Titania away to prepare for the epithalamium in honour of Theseus, where they can now bless his house 'to all fair prosperity'.

Oberon also prophesies the weddings of the 'pairs of faithful lovers', who have yet to wake. Sure enough, when Theseus's hunting horns are wound to arouse them, the couples find their love quarrels have also been resolved, because Demetrius now loves Helena. We do not know if his new love for Helena is the effect of the love-juice, left on his eyes deliberately by Oberon, or is a restoration of what he felt before:

> To her, my lord,
> Was I betrothed ere I saw Hermia;
> But like a sickness did I loathe this food.
> But, as in health come to my natural taste,
> Now I do wish it, love it, long for it,
> And will for evermore be true to it.
>
> (IV.1.170–175)

His experience is very like Titania's, and the repetition of the word 'loathe' helps to underline the similarity and to show the closeness of love and loathing. Perhaps Bottom should roll in his sleep at this moment, to bring the parallel to our notice. For the moment he sleeps on. Theseus quickly exploits the opportunity to override Egeus's opposition in what might be considered a high-handed manner, and to end all possibility of dispute, by marrying off the couples.

As Theseus leads Hippolyta away, the air of finality may seem somewhat contrived to a modern audience, but it is typical of several of Shakespeare comedies where loose ends are tied up with unconvincing speed. In *As You Like It*, four couples' troth is plighted at the end and a new character comes on to announce that the villain has suddenly been converted from his evil ways. At the end of *The Winter's Tale*, a tragic situation is suddenly resolved happily and the characters are paired off and led rapidly away by the king. However, in each case, there is some exception to the general joy; in *As You Like It*, the solitary character of Jaques deliberately spurns mirth and celebration, deciding to live in self-imposed banishment; while in *The Winter's Tale* the happy ending is marred by the knowledge that two significant characters are dead through no fault of their own. At the end of *Twelfth Night*, another important Shakespeare comedy, the harmonious happy ending is modified by the fury of the character Malvolio, who has been tricked and abused, and who makes his exit threatening revenge.

These comparisons should alert us to the typical shape of Shakespeare's comic endings. Happiness and harmony are restored through devices which are as rapidly enacted as the deaths which bring some of the tragedies to their swift and fatal conclusions. Yet the happiness is incomplete: some note of bitterness or sadness is sounded that affects the final tone of the play.

With these endings in mind, let us return to *A Midsummer Night's Dream* and examine the significance of Bottom in the final scenes of the play. After Theseus's all but conclusive exit, the four lovers are left to reflect on the strangeness of their experience. This reflective quality characterises much of the ending. Demetrius is the most expressive of them in describing the feeling of remoteness and unreality they experience:

> These things seem small and undistinguishable,
> Like far-off mountains turnèd into clouds.

> (IV.1.186–187)

> Are you sure
> That we are awake? It seems to me
> That yet we sleep, we dream.

> (IV.1.191–193)

But finally convinced by the recollection of Theseus's summons, he concludes:

Why, then, we are awake. Let's follow him,
And by the way let's recount our dreams.

(IV.1.197–198)

And now Bottom wakes, momentarily returning straight to the moment in rehearsal when he was 'transformed'. Then he remembers. And the question an actor has to answer is *what* exactly does he remember? Only fragments of what has happened remain with him, but in his attempt to express his blurred recollection, he achieves an eloquence that is strangely moving:

> I have had a most rare vision. I have had a dream past the wit of man to say what dream it was. Man is but an ass if he go about to expound this dream. Methought I was — there is no man can tell what. Methought I was — and methought I had — but man is but a patched fool if he will offer to say what methought I had.
>
> (IV.1.203–208)

The references to 'ass' and 'fool' bring comic irony to the speech. Most actors in the role use gestures to comic effect here, indicating the long ears, nose and hair of the ass's head, but the emphasis on wonderment and on the word 'man' bring a biblical grandeur to the speech, which is carried through in the next lines, a parody of a passage from 1 Corinthians 2:9, 'Eye hath not seen, nor ear heard, neither have entered into the heart of man, the things which God hath prepared for them that love him.'

From biblical language, Bottom moves to the idea of poetry, intending Peter Quince to write a ballad of his dream, a typical Shakespearean device to remind the audience that they are watching a play which *is*, in part, a dramatic ballad about his dream. The actor may decide to play for laughs, emphasising Bottom's incorrigible self-confidence, but the scope is there to extend the sense of wonder and to reveal layers of deeper significance. 'It shall be called "Bottom's dream",' he says, meaning first of all because it is his dream, but then he adds, 'because it hath no bottom'. This carries a triple meaning which must be given time to sink in. A 'bottom' is a tool of the weaver's trade — a core onto which the skein of thread is wound — hence his name. Thus, he may mean that the dream has no centre, or perhaps no thread, but he also plays on the more usual meanings of the word. The dream has no bottom — it has no depth, is shallow and meaningless, *or* it is of immeasurable depth. This simple, foolish line resonates powerfully, making us wonder at the meaning of Bottom's experience, the effect of the dream on him, the meaning of dreams in general, and leads us to contemplate simplicity, foolishness and innocence as such.

Having awoken to the moment of his enchantment, then remembered his dream, Bottom now begins to recollect hazily what the future holds, as he plans to sing the ballad 'in the latter end of a play before the Duke. Peradventure, to make it the more gracious, I shall sing it at her death.' He leaves, presumably to look for Peter Quince and the others. Harold Brooks, editor of the Arden edition, has suggested that 'a play' is the correct reading, not 'the play' because his mind is still blurred, and that 'her death' is an as yet vague projection of himself as hero with the heroine in transition in his mind between Titania and Thisbe.

While the major drama is over, we are now reminded of Bottom's all-important role in his comrades' venture. A brief scene follows in which the other workmen lament his absence, a scene just long enough for his re-entrance to have some impact, and for us to re-acquaint ourselves with their slow but steadfast ways, and their affection and admiration for 'sweet Bully Bottom' (IV.2.18). Then he returns, in a delightful parody of a hero's homecoming, still unable to explain the 'wonders' he has encountered. Easier by far to push on with the good news that their play is preferred (short-listed, but not yet finally selected).

And so we come to the final Act and scene, which, unusually for Shakespeare, adds nothing to the plot. What does the presentation of *Pyramus and Thisbe* — and in particular Bottom's performance in it — contribute to the play as a whole? There are parallels with the main story — the forbidden marriage (Thisbe's to Pyramus, Hermia's to Lysander) and the escape. Also, just as Oberon and Puck have made fun of the mortals, now the nobles make fun of the lesser mortals. It is usual, in production, for every stop to be pulled out to make the parody of tragedy funny for the audience. However, it may be that we have learnt enough of Bottom to see the performance from his point of view, as well as that of the courtiers. One of the reasons Theseus has asked for entertainment is to receive such offerings as his subjects make to him. When Hippolyta complains that the actors 'can do nothing in this kind', he retorts: 'The kinder we, to give them thanks for nothing' (V.1.88–89). He tells her of occasions when he has 'picked a welcome' from speakers who completely broke down, because of stage fright. He introduces the theme of love in a completely different way from how it has been treated so far, as the love between a subject and a ruler:

> Love, therefore, and tongue-tied simplicity
> In least speak most, to my capacity.

(V.1.104–105)

Against this idealistic viewpoint must be set the more materialistic motivation of the players themselves, that if they perform well, they may win a grant of 'sixpence a day'. However one balances these points of view, both suggest a high degree of tension and apprehension in the players.

In the event, nothing in fact goes wrong with the performance from the point of view of the players. And yet they fail, and make themselves ridiculous. By the end, even Theseus can find nothing to commend except:

> This palpable-gross play hath well beguiled
> The heavy gait of night. Sweet friends to bed.

(V.1.357–358)

In other words, they have filled the time before the three marriages will be consummated.

But to reach a final balance in the play, with its interlocking groups of characters, the players of *Pyramus and Thisbe* should not appear more ridiculous than the mortals have appeared to Puck. Hermia's love and Helena's might have ended in tragedy. What we feel in the final moments of the play-within-play should be as close to the pain of tragedy as Bottom is to grasping the importance of his dream. What should happen is that we laugh with Theseus's court at the simplicity of the actors, and the foolishness of their script, but that we are also moved by their innocence and honest intentions. Perhaps Bottom speaks Pyramus's last speech with a glimmering of awareness of the beautiful woman (Titania) whom he nearly possessed, but who died to him:

> Sweet moon, I thank thee for thy sunny beams;

I thank thee, Moon, for shining now so bright;
For by thy gracious, golden, glittering beams
I trust to take of truest Thisbe sight.

(V.1.264–267)

Theseus tells us:

Lovers and madmen have such seething brains,
Such shaping fantasies, that apprehend
More than cool reason ever comprehends.

(V.1.4–6)

Bottom is neither a lover nor a madman; he is a foolish and well-meaning clown. But which is the more ridiculous? And what happens if a foolish clown does play the lover? These are the questions raised by this most lovable of Shakespeare's characters.

AFTERTHOUGHTS

1

Do you believe that Demetrius's love for Helena at the end of the play is the effect of the love-juice or 'a restoration of what he felt before' (page 90)?

2

What implications does Devlin suggest for Bottom's explanation of what he will call his dream (pages 92–93)?

3

Do you agree that the final Act of *A Midsummer Night's Dream* 'adds nothing to the plot' (page 93)?

4

How would you answer the questions raised by Devlin in the final paragraph of this essay?

Josie Alwyn

Josie Alwyn teaches literature at the West Sussex Institute of Higher Education and is an experienced A-level examiner.

ESSAY

The artful disorder of the dream world

A Midsummer Night's Dream is both pattern and process. In the theatre we become involved with the unfolding process of the drama and so absorbed in the enchantment of movement, light, colour, sound and the suspension of disbelief that we fail to notice an underlying choreography. However, if we could freeze the process at any point we would see an intricate patterning of figures, not simply a stage pattern, but a poetic pattern of associations that refract meaning just as a diamond, turning, refracts light from its myriad facets.

In this essay I wish to focus on these patterns for it seems to me that the three great settings of *A Midsummer Night's Dream* — Athens, The Wood and The Wedding Night — are like three great tapestries which can be understood emblematically and which define each other by contrast. Let us look at Athens first, in order to clarify the contrary realm of The Wood.

When we explore emblematic meaning we look, not for veracity, but for patterns of association. This is straightforward in the world of Athens: 'the city' in literature traditionally represents order, civility and reason, and Athens has a special place in that tradition as the cradle of Western philosophy and, thus, the seat of classical Reason. Our identification of Athens with 'Reason' and 'Order' is confirmed by our introduction to Theseus and Hippolyta. Theseus, according to legend, was the first to vanquish the warring tribes of Greece and to unite them as one nation state under his government in Athens. Here he is on the verge of marrying Hippolyta who, as Queen of the Amazons, represents one of the vanquished tribes; as an Amazon woman warrior she represents a race of man-haters who subvert the dominance of male reason; furthermore, as the female principal she represents irrational, subversive elements in both human nature and Mother Nature. In the play's opening we therefore have a multilayered emblem where each layer enforces the same message: Theseus, the epitome of male reason and order, stands here on the verge of controlling all the potentially irrational elements in his nation, his social hierarchy and himself through his marriage to Hippolyta, whom he has brought within the citadel of Reason.

This exposition sets up an emblematic pattern which is repeated through all the classes of Athenian society: in Egeus and then in Quince we see the heads of microcosmic societies attempting to bring irrational elements under their control. Egeus wants to control his daughter's irrational desires within the laws of arranged marriage. Quince attempts to contain the unruly concerns of the workmen within the courtly conventions of a love tragedy.

By repeating this structural motif throughout each class of the Athenian hierarchy we are given the sense of a coherent body politic (from the Head of State to the literal Bottom) and we are also given the clear sense of a deep flaw in this cool and rational social order; a flaw which has to do with the very rigidity of its ordering.

The wall that separates Pyramus and Thisbe is only the most visible of many walls in *A Midsummer Night's Dream*: walls of prejudice, walls of convention, walls of law that separate characters from their heart's desire. Every situation we meet in Athens has to do with love and marriage, but only marriage is presented as an institution fulfilling a reasonable function. The marriage of Theseus is a symbol of government, his husbandly control of Hippolyta representing both his control of the nation state and his subjugation of his own irrational desires. For Egeus, likewise, marriage has nothing to do with the fulfilment of love but everything to do with the dutiful submission of children to their father's power. Hermia and Lysander are separated by the flint-hard wall of marriage law as surely as Pyramus and Thisbe are divided by the wall between their father's neighbouring estates. Having no experience, the young lovers can only refer to the traditions of romantic love for counsel: 'For aught that I could ever read,/ Could ever hear by tale or history,/ The course of true love never did run smooth' (I.1.132–134), says Lysander and, according to the book, lovers like Hermia and Lysander are doomed to a tragic end. In Athens, then, marriage is reasonable but loveless, while love is fatal; the rigid walls of law and of convention suffocate natural desires.

Our introduction to the 'mechanicals' illuminates this 'flaw' from yet another perspective, for the confining walls here are those of dramatic convention. We watch Bottom's exuberant creativity pushing against those walls of convention in all directions: he cannot be contained by one role but wishes to play *all* the parts; he is insubordinate to his director and almost impossible for Quince to control; when the desire to play a tyrant overwhelms him he cannot control himself; 'tragic' speeches flow from him, and when he says that he will move his audience to 'storms' of tears we believe him. We know they will be tears of *laughter*, but Bottom's passionate love of acting will overwhelm us as surely as it overwhelms him and will have us helplessly falling off our seats with most improper laughter. Here we have a different form of passionate love: Bottom's desire is for fulfilment through artistic creativity, whereas the lovers' desire seeks fulfilment through procreativity. The Elizabethan word which includes both nuances of desire is 'fancy'; a word debased over the centuries and now almost extinct but once indicative of a powerful state of passionate desire:

> Tell me where is fancy bred,
> Or in the heart, or in the head?
>
> (*Merchant of Venice*, III.2.63–64)

The lovers' fancy breeds in their hearts, whereas it is Bottom's head that is full of fantasies.

The great tapestry of Athens, then, depicts an orthodox order so rigidly controlled by reason that there is no room for desire to change anything. It is human to act on those things we feel most passionate about and here we see passionate desires so stifled that the most engaging, 'fanciful' characters can achieve nothing in the city and escape its confines — Hermia and Lysander elope, Helena's passionate jealousy leads her and Demetrius to follow, and Bottom takes his passion for play-acting to the wood for rehearsal. 'Fancy', then, is the theme which picks up and guides the thread to weave the world of *A Midsummer Night's Dream*. Let us turn now to the next phase of that process: to the wood beyond the city walls.

From the earliest classical traditions 'the city' has been compared with 'the country' to expose the virtues and vices of both, and Shakespeare draws on that tradition in juxtaposing 'Athens' with 'The Wood'. When Demetrius declares, 'And here am I, and wood within this wood' (II.1.192) we are directed to a play on 'wood' and 'woo'd' (for Helena chasing Demetrius reverses the roles) and also to the Elizabethan association of 'wood' with 'mad'. If Athens represents rational order, is the wood its antithesis: the place of madness and disorder? Our experience of the wood in performance is certainly a giddy sense of the free play of confusions. We are never sure whether the wood is a place or a state of mind, a supernatural realm or a representation of night, and through this uncertainty Shakespeare creates in us the mercurial, elusive condition of dreaming; so that later, just like Bottom waking from his dream and the lovers waking from theirs, we find that we too have a powerful experience that we can neither describe nor explain away, and the magic of it remains.

For Shakespeare to create this condition in his audience suggests a high degree of artistry and, indeed, if we turn our attention back to the underlying pattern we see an intricate choreographing of disordered relationships mirroring the ordered relationships set up in Athens. Here, as there, the primary focus is on love and marriage but the contrast begins the moment we enter the wood to find ourselves suddenly in the dark amid the servants who define the parameters of this 'other' realm for us:

> PUCK How now, spirit; whither wander you?
> FAIRY Over hill, over dale,
>   Thorough bush, thorough briar,
>   Over park, over pale,

Thorough flood, thorough fire —
I do wander everywhere
Swifter than the moon's sphere

(II.1.1–5)

These may be the 'lower orders' of the fairy world but they are the opposite of the corporeal craftsmen (the lower orders of Athens) we have just left: look how this wandering spirit can transgress all the rigid hierarchies set up in Athens, flying over hills and valleys, across garden fences and walls, unimpeded by the elements; and while even Theseus is governed by the moon's phases, this fairy moves beyond them. The trochaic trimeter and the feminine end-rhymes convey the speed and transgressive power here and directly contrast the measured iambic pentameter of Theseus's introductory blank verse in Act I. The Fairy Queen's servant is from chivalric romance but Puck, on the other hand, is that 'lob of spirits' (II.1.16) from English folk-lore, who is more connected with the transgressions and liberation of carnival. Through these fairy servants we first see the wood in contrast to Athens's ceremonials and hierarchies as a place of process, fluidity and transformation.

Whereas Theseus and Hippolyta had been introduced like classical gods — framed together, statuesque, calmly awaiting their solemn wedding ceremony — Oberon and Titania are a long-married couple who now enter unceremoniously from opposite sides of the stage and immediately set to arguing. In this they enact the opposite of a proper Elizabethan marriage. First, passion rules them, not reason: sexual passions and jealousies, adulterous disloyalties, anger, pride and possessiveness. Secondly, there is no home to contain Titania as a 'housewife' and for which Oberon could be the 'hous-band', for the fairies wander freely over the world. Thirdly, Oberon has no conventional control over his wife — he does not win her back with his sword, like Theseus, but resorts to underhand conspiracy to get his way. Moreover, the conspiracy involves Titania possibly committing adultery with an ass, so that Oberon turns *himself* into a cuckold of the basest sort (cuckolds were the biggest buffoons of Elizabethan humour). Even their names produce a comically reversed image of the ideal husband and wife; for Oberon, the king of the woods, is traditionally only a metre tall, while Titania's name associated her with the enormous Titanic gods. Yet Titania is later described as small enough to sleep in a jewelled snake skin and while she sleeps Oberon seems to tower over her in malevolence as he chants his dark incantations. Oberon shifts continually between the foolish and the powerful, between malevolence and benign providence, and this shifting quality is true of all aspects of the wood. Where Athens was defined by rigid oppositions, nothing seems fixed here: as in a dream, we begin to lose the principles by which we can order anything.

It is the lovers who came to deepest confusion in the wood; their fervent vows in Athens were clichés from the book of romance and now we watch their conventional language coming unstuck and falling apart as they lose their way in the dark. Lysander has to admit that 'to speak troth — I have forgot our way' (II.2.42), and it is not only their path, but also the honourable way to behave, that he has forgotten. Now he tries to use the power of romantic language to corrupt Hermia's innocence, and the 'lies', which are phonetically associated with his name, now fly free so that lies and contradictions become part of his language: 'For lying so, Hermia, I do not lie' (II.2.58). This disordering of language, truth and meaning happens to all the lovers as they undergo a carefully patterned disordering 'dance' of different and increasingly quarrelsome partners, until late in the night they are as lost and miserable as schoolchildren: their courtly language is reduced to silent misery, their individual identities are dissolved in tears, and they wander their separate ways through the wood, having achieved the reverse of their aim of fulfilling their heart's desire.

In the wood the young lover's real and painful experience is a 'fond pageant' (III.2.114) for Puck; while, in a further outrageous reversal, Bottom goes to the wood to *play* the part of a lover and becomes instead really beloved by the Fairy Queen herself. Thus, the humblest member of society is set up higher than even the king for, in a fantastic reversal of courtly love, the highest lady here dotes upon and kneels before the 'courteous knight'. As Bottom represents the 'body' in this play he is the only character to be physically transformed: he literally takes on the head of an ass, reversing the Athenian focus on the head of Reason. There is a curious ambivalence here; it is wonderfully comic and it has pathos, too (for Bottom is a most 'courtly' ass) but there is also an echo of the Minotaur (which Theseus slew) in the stage image of a man with a beast's head and darker implications of the bestial passions with which donkeys are also associated; there is charming innocence in Bottom being the only mortal to play with the fairies and yet those fairies are also supernaturally weird. In these ways Bottom and Titania's love affair slips and slides and shifts between the sublime and the ridiculous, the animal and the refined, monstrous fear and comic delight. Their relationship, at the heart of the disordered world, is a shattered mirror image of everything an orthodox relationship between man and woman should be and it crystallises the whole night the wood as a dramatic tapestry depicting how the free play of passions brings chaos to all orthodox order:

> Kings, Queenes, Lords, Ladies, Knights and Damsels gente
> Were heap'd together with the vulgar sort
> And mingled with the raskal rabblement
> Without respect of person of port
> To show Dan Cupid's power and great effort
> (*The Faerie Queene*, Book 3, Canto XI, lines 46–51)

This is taken from a description of a tapestry in Spenser's *Faerie Queene* which was published at the same time as *A Midsummer Night's Dream* and has a similar focus on love and marriage; it may well have been in Shakespeare's mind as he created the *Dream* world. There are other associations, too; in the daylight world of Athens, Bottom is a weaver and moreover 'bottom' is a term used in weaving for the bobbin carrying the weft thread, which is woven to and fro. When Puck decides to be an 'actor' in the 'hempen homespuns' play (III.1.70–73), he uses Bottom very much like the instrument associated with his name, for Puck picks him up, spins him round and proceeds to weave him up into a love fantasy that is like 'a dream come true'. So, while Bottom is the weaver of the everyday world, it is Puck who weaves the dreams of night. Puck's 'director' is Oberon; but Puck is as insubordinate an actor as Bottom is with Quince, and here he tangles the threads that Oberon asked him to weave, and achieves, not the harmonious resolution Oberon intended, but something very like the chaos that Cupid works in the world. Is Puck, then, the Cupid of Shakespeare's fanciful world? Is the 'lob of spirits' the English equivalent of Venus's naughty boy? If the idea has any credence it must be comic, for it places Oberon in the position of Venus, and who, then, is Titania's 'lovely' changeling boy (II.1.22–23)?

What is clear in Athens and the wood is the representation of a thesis (the rigid inadequacy of a rationale that excludes desire) followed by an antithesis (the chaos caused by the unbounded free play of desire). As Bottom observes; 'reason and love keep little company together nowadays — the more the pity that some honest neighbours will not make them friends' (III.1.136–138). Shakespeare, however, does have a device to 'make them friends' and just as we have absorbed this spectacle of Chaos the weaving process begins again.

The whole of Act IV trembles on the brink of dawn and enacts a magical harmonising process as Oberon and Puck together untangle the confusions of the night and weave all the different figures together in a truly harmonious pattern to leave on the shores of morning. The lovers enact this harmony as they awake; their language is now neither rigidly conventional nor disordered by overwhelming passion, there is a harmony now between reason and experience: 'truly would I speak' (IV.1.148), says Lysander with simple clarity. Theseus's rationale is softened by this sight and he sanctions the marriage of true lovers and brings about the wonderful synthesis that ends the play.

I leave you to investigate fully the harmony of The Wedding Night: it is a tapestry of concord in which every aspect of order and disorder seems to be balanced and harmonised. As Bottom assures Theseus, 'the wall is down that parted their fathers' (V.1.342–343) and, in so doing, he enacts the harmonising of a social order in which the 'Bottom' can converse happily with the 'Head'. Other walls are down too: the lovers are united with their heart's desire and their marriages represent the harmonious continuation of social order; so love tragedy becomes love comedy and the 'tedious epilogue' is replaced by joyful dancing; finally Theseus acknowledges 'fairy time' and the immortal elements bless the house of the sleeping mortals. The Wedding Night suggests many of the harmonious qualities of midsummer night itself; for here, traditionally, time passing meets a point of infinity, so that all midsummer nights past, present and future are gathered up and dilate into the timeless dance of life. Process and pattern melt into each other here at the still point of the turning world:

> In that open field
> If you do not come too close, if you do not come too close,
> On a summer midnight, you can hear the music
> Of the weak pipe and the little drum
> And see them dancing around the bonfire
> The association of man and woman
> In daunsinge, signifying matrimonie —
> A dignified and commodios sacrament.
> Two and two, necessarye coniunction,
> Holding eche other by the hand or the arm
> Whiche betokeneth concorde.

(T S Eliot, Four Quartets, 'East Coker', Part I)

AFTERTHOUGHTS

1

What do you understand by 'A Midsummer Night's Dream is both pattern and process' (page 97)?

2

Do you agree with Alwyn's description of the 'many walls' in A Midsummer Night's Dream (pages 98–99)?

3

Why does Alwyn suggest that 'We are never sure whether the wood is a place or a state of mind' (page 100)? Do you agree?

4

Explain the relevance to Alwyn's argument of the quotation from Spenser's The Faerie Queene (page 103).

Christopher McCullough

Christopher McCullough is Lecturer in Drama at the University of Exeter. He is editor of the journal Studies in Theatre Production.

ESSAY

Inner stages: levels of illusion in *A Midsummer Night's Dream*

> All that is fine in the play, was lost in the representation. The spirit was evaporated, the genius was fled; but the spectacle was fine: it was that which saved the play.
>
> (William Hazlitt, *The Examiner*, 1816)[1]

Hazlitt's praise of the stage spectacle of *A Midsummer Night's Dream* (an operatic version) in 1816 was, I am sure, ironic; his contention was that 'Poetry and the stage do not agree together'. The message of the word, the poetry, was destroyed for him by the excess of the spectacle. This view of Shakespeare's plays has been given wide currency since the eighteenth century and of course forms one of the underlying principles behind the inclusion of Shakespeare's plays on A-level English Literature syllabuses (as opposed to Theatre Arts syllabuses). There is a certain justification in this point of view. At least the received

---

[1] *In The Round Table* (London, 1969), p. 61.

text, scholarly reconstruction of a theatrical event though it might be, is a concrete encoding of the poetry of the play, capable of being read without hindrance by stage action or spectacle.

However, the kind of pictorial spectacle referred to in this production of 1816 was of a convention that was not prevalent at the time of the play's original context of making in the late 1590s. The popular conception even today is that of elaborate woodland scenery populated by live animals and exotic fairies of varying sizes, owing more in inspiration to the imagination of a Victorian children's illustrator than they do to the Elizabethan mind. The Elizabethan stage, while not being entirely devoid of visual imagery, was almost certainly not engaged in the elaborate pictorial forms of scenography that emerged gradually throughout the seventeenth century, reaching their high point in the late nineteenth and early twentieth centuries. The important question to pursue in this area of analysis concerns not the rejection of visual contextualisation in staging plays like *A Midsummer Night's Dream*, but precisely what forms of visual realisation best suit the play's theatrical potential. The fact that the play's fantastical conventions confront notional stage realism does seem to form the basis of a possible critical focus. The human characters move between differing levels of consciousness; the court of Athens, which is the yardstick of harsh 'reality' in the world of the play's fiction, gives way to the alternative fantastical reality of the woodland.

The play operates on a number of levels of reality distinguished primarily by two specific physical locations: the court and the woodland. These two worlds are very different; the court, the harsh and violent world of human beings — in some ways the world of the Elizabethan audience — and the woodland the world of fantastical imagination. The woodland isn't, as many directors suppose, a world of total freedom and escape from the harsh realities of the court, but is more a world where the conventions of the everyday world are lifted (rather as happens in the theatre) and replaced, not by anarchy, but by alternative conventions, manifest in the play's imagery as magic. It is these two worlds that require, if the play is to achieve a theatrical realisation, a visual code that makes distinct for an audience (of whatever period) the two levels of fictional consciousness. Is this where the problems start — in a disjunction between the idea of the poetry of literature and that of the poetry of theatre?

The events of the first Act are in the main concerned with the social and emotional condition of the humans in the play and with the depiction of the values of the Athenian court. In effect we are introduced to three levels of Athenian society: the men of the ruling class, the women of the ruling class and, finally, the artisans of that city. This picture of Athens is drawn from diverse sources and in no way may be seen as a historical reconstruction of classical Athens. The city and court are drawn from elements of myth, legend, drama and local English folklore, as are the characters of the play. Immediately we can see that to attempt, either in the mind's eye of the reader or in the scenography of a stage production, a kind of historical verisimilitude would only lead to the confusions that abound in stage interpretations of Elizabethan dramas. The Elizabethan audience should have had little problem in understanding this world of the Athenian court as being a world of fiction when we consider how the stage emphasis was towards an overt or self-reflexive theatricality. That is to say that the Elizabethan actors, aided by their performance script and physical stage conditions, would have had no inhibitions about declaring their *art*; unlike many modern actors whose cultural ideology compels them toward a notion that they are not *acting* but *being* when portraying characters on stage.

Our first introduction to this contrived world is to the Duke Theseus and his betrothed, Queen Hippolyta. This world is violent and oppressive, where an exact retribution is meted out on those persons, both men and women, who do not conform to its accepted values. Hippolyta, we learn on the first page, was not won by love and tenderness but by Theseus's sword doing her injuries (I.1.16–17). And the wedding itself is to be carried out 'With pomp, with triumph, and with revelling' (I.1.18–19). Whose triumph? What follows does little to alleviate our concern for the plight of women in this court. The central characters are four young people, of high birth, caught in the familiar tangled web of Elizabethan comedy: Lysander loves Hermia; Helena loves Demetrius who, although he once professed love to her (I.1.107), has rejected her in favour of Hermia. What further complicates the issue is the fact that Hermia's father, Egeus, favours Demetrius rather than Lysander and is willing to demand the harshness of the law of this Athens if his will is not met:

> As she is mine, I may dispose of her;
> Which shall be either to this gentleman
> Or to her death, according to our law
> Immediately provided in that case.

(I.1.42–45)

This isn't the only recourse at his disposal: the Duke offers another, hardly less repressive alternative, that of her entering a nunnery for the rest of her life (I.1.70). As a consequence, Hermia and Lysander choose to flee from this oppressive society, not to the woodland of Oberon and Titania, but to another 'real' world less harsh than that of Theseus's court: the house of Lysander's aunt, some seven leagues remote from Athens (I.1.159). The wood is intended to be their initial meeting place, not their ultimate objective, but of course the discord of that world disrupts their progress by supplanting it with its own illusory reality.

The woodland of *A Midsummer Night's Dream* is undoubtedly a different world in both the literary and the theatrical readings of the play. A cultural leap of the imagination is required on the part of the reader/audience in order that the rules by which this new world operates may be assimilated. There is a sense that the woodland is an overtly theatrical world; theatrical in the sense that it is a place that operates by disturbing people's perceptions of themselves and the world around them. This sounds rather sinister and would be so if it were not for the fantastical and comic level upon which this all takes place. The confusions of the lovers and the 'mechanicals', fantastical in their origin and comic in their outcome — which is not to deny their pain — stand in sharp contrast to the oppression of the court in the first Act. The comic aspect serves as a mediator between the harsh male reason of the court and the illusions of the wood. In the wood, male reason (so dominant in the court values that the lovers carry with them) fails to constrain the emotions that are given free rein by the actions of Oberon and Puck, and is thus undermined. It may be possible to see the fairy world of illusion and fantasy functioning as a metaphor for theatre itself; for theatre, when not restricted by modern naturalistic conventions, may challenge perceptions of a social order that attempts to naturalise itself into a permanent transcendental order. In *A Midsummer Night's Dream* it is very difficult to say, 'life's like that' because the play does not readily lend itself to the constraint of the single view of reality. Puck's last speech, the final speech of the play, delivered directly to the audience, is an admission of theatricality; his world and that of Oberon and Titania is the world of theatre:

> If we shadows have offended,
> Think but this, and all is mended:
> That you have but slumbered here
> While these visions did appear.
>
> (V.1.413–416)

This is not to suggest that the alternative stage world is necessarily to be dismissed as 'a weak and idle theme' (V.1.417). Rather, we have the possibility of remembering how easily and effectively these insubstantial images may challenge the rigidity of the court's values, and of remembering that the court itself is only a construct of the shadowy world of the stage. The ultimate function of theatrical illusion is to affect the audience's perception of both stage worlds and not to limit the theatrical experience to a satisfying observation of the tying up of loose ends in the fictional world of the play. Theseus's 'reason' is inadequate to the task of fully comprehending the experience of the wood as described to him by the lovers:

> Lovers and madmen have such seething brains,
> Such shaping fantasies, that apprehend
> More than cool reason ever comprehends.
>
> (V.1.4–6)

The escape to the wood is often interpreted as a retreat to nature; a retreat to a notion of the proper order of things, based on the rhythm of seasons and the working of nature. However, in *A Midsummer Night's Dream* the image contained in the metaphor of the wood could hardly be further from a concept of uncorrupted nature within which both humans and animals will respond to a supposed natural rhythm of life. The domain of

Oberon and Titania is one where they rule every aspect and condition of life in an entirely unpredictable and unreasonable manner, and in which, it would seem, even the weather is created by the current relationship between the two creatures (II.1.88–100). But it is the very fantastical and overt artificiality of this world that distances it from the dangerously familiar harshness of the world of the court. Rather than fleeing to some notion of the natural order and flow of nature, the lovers and the artisans are moving into an artificial world where the imagination, in outrunning conventional reason, may create confusion. Alternatively it may encourage new insights; adults have a habit of marginalising adolescent perceptions as confusion!

The lovers and Bottom emerge from the wood at dawn changed in a variety of ways. In the case of the lovers, the change in their own perceptions of their interrelationships may be seen as being merely on the level of the expedient. The reaffirmation of Hermia and Lysander's coupling and the transfer of Demetrius's affections from Hermia back to Helena keep the narrative neat. The value for the audience, however, is in observing, in the fantastical (that is Acts II, III and IV), the potential for constructing modes of conduct that challenge ideologically the patriarchal reason of Athens.

Bottom's awakening from his 'dream' is significant both in terms of the fictional character's progression and in the manner by which the theatre addresses itself to its audience. The change in the lovers takes place entirely within the fiction of the performance and is signified by a poetic language. The articulation of Bottom's awakening, however, occurs as a direct address to the audience, a theatrical device by which Bottom — or rather the actor playing Bottom — may sidestep for the moment the character in order to enter into a cultural conspiracy with the audience. This stage device is further emphasised by Bottom speaking in prose, and marks the first opportunity for us to concentrate on a single figure that represents a class other than that of the Athenian court: a pre-working-class artisan. Bottom, left alone on stage, is momentarily freed from the class tensions that curb his exuberant rhetorical energies, invoked by the need to produce a theatrical piece politically acceptable to the court of Theseus (I.2.74–76). He has the sense of something, only half remembered, that defies conventional reasoning: 'I have had a dream past the wit of man to say what dream it was' (IV.1.203–204). Bottom's thoughts are confused as he grasps for the memory, and his mixing of the functions of his sensory organs, rather than making him look foolish, distances him from the assertive males of the phallocentric court (IV.1.208–211). This is a theatrical moment when language (the poet's art) and spectacle (the actor's craft) combine in order to illuminate the audience's perception of reality, rather than, as Hazlitt believed, disrupting that possibility.

So far, the potential audience has been presented with two significant levels of reality occurring within the fictional stage world. Act V brings about a more complicated situation, whereby the audience in the theatre observes a 'surrogate' audience on stage watching a play performance occurring within the main play. Can there be three levels of 'reality' within A Midsummer Night's Dream and what bearing does that possibility have on the play's theatrical structure? The audience in the theatre, the 'surrogate' audience and the artisans' actual performance of Pyramus and Thisbe are dramatic and theatrical elements that combine to relate to each other on a dialectical level. That means that the differences are not antagonistic (in the way that Hazlitt found when he observed that spectacle disrupted the poetry), but work in such a way that when juxtaposed they offer new ways of looking at what we perceive reality to be. The members of the surrogate audience, as fictions themselves, do nothing to suggest to the audience that they are anything other than real, whereas the players/artisans are continually concerned to remind the audience (surrogate) of their theatricality, for fear of violent retribution lest they fright the ladies (I.2.74). However, the structure of the performance of Pyramus and Thisbe is delineated by the surrogate audience's commentary on the 'stage' action of the artisans and, by so doing, the members of the surrogate audience are not allowed to become invisible and almost blend in with the real audience, but are foregrounded as commentators. By becoming active participants in the artisans' theatre-making, they are prevented from being subsumed into an illusion that would reinforce the idea that this is how the real world is: unchangeably cruel and oppressive. The point and counterpoint between the playing of Pyramus and Thisbe and the commentary of its critical surrogate audience does not liberate the lives of the artisans any more than the entry into the world of the woodland changes the status quo for the lives of lovers. There will be other Hermias and Helenas with fates bound by the wills of dukes and fathers. The play's theatrical practice does not work in that way. The discourse of the play centres on the interplay between dramatic language and theatrical spectacle. What emerges in performance should not be a conflict between the semantics of poetry and the action of spectacle, but a synthesis produced by the dialectical juxtaposition of the two. It is the audience sitting in the auditorium who are offered the possibility of learning from their observation of this structural interplay and its effect on the content of the drama.

AFTERTHOUGHTS

1

Do you agree with Hazlitt's contention that 'Poetry and the stage do not agree together' (page 107)?

2

What sort of set would *you* prefer for the woodland in *A Midsummer Night's Dream*?

3

What three 'levels of 'reality'' (page 113) does McCullough identify in this essay?

4

What do you understand by 'a synthesis produced by the dialectical juxtaposition of the two' (page 114)?

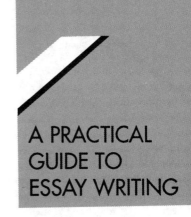

INTRODUCTION

First, a word of warning. Good essays are the product of a
creative engagement with literature. So never try to restrict
your studies to what you think will be 'useful in the exam'.
Ironically, you will restrict your grade potential if you do.

This doesn't mean, of course, that you should ignore the
basic skills of essay writing. When you read critics, make a
conscious effort to notice *how* they communicate their ideas. The
guidelines that follow offer advice of a more explicit kind. But
they are no substitute for practical experience. It is never easy
to express ideas with clarity and precision. But the more often
you tackle the problems involved and experiment to find your
own voice, the more fluent you will become. So practise writing
essays as often as possible.

HOW TO PLAN AN ESSAY

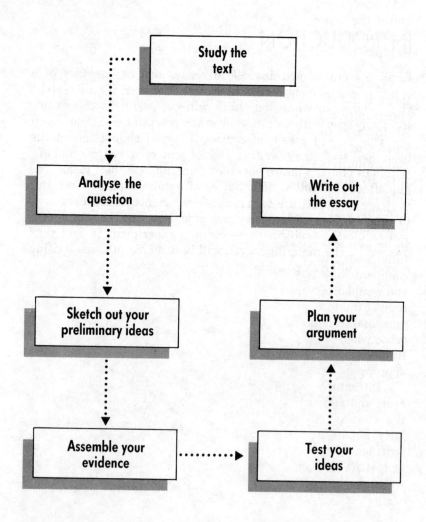

Study the text

Analyse the question

Sketch out your preliminary ideas

Assemble your evidence

Test your ideas

Plan your argument

Write out the essay

Study the text

The first step in writing a good essay is to get to know the set text well. Never write about a text until you are fully familiar with it. Even a discussion of the opening chapter of a novel, for example, should be informed by an understanding of the book as a whole. Literary texts, however, are by their very nature complex and on a first reading you are bound to miss many significant features. Re-read the book with care, if possible more than once. Look up any unfamiliar words in a good dictionary and if the text you are studying was written more than a few decades ago, consult the *Oxford English Dictionary* to find out whether the meanings of any terms have shifted in the intervening period.

Good books are difficult to put down when you first read them. But a more leisurely second or third reading gives you the opportunity to make notes on those features you find significant. An index of characters and events is often useful, particularly when studying novels with a complex plot or time scheme. The main aim, however, should be to record your *responses* to the text. By all means note, for example, striking images. But be sure to add *why* you think them striking. Similarly, record any thoughts you may have on interesting comparisons with other texts, puzzling points of characterisation, even what you take to be aesthetic blemishes. The important thing is to annotate fully and adventurously. The most seemingly idiosyncratic comment may later lead to a crucial area of discussion which you would otherwise have overlooked. It helps to have a working copy of the text in which to mark up key passages and jot down marginal comments (although obviously these practices are taboo when working with library, borrowed or valuable copies!). But keep a fuller set of notes as well and organise these under appropriate headings.

Literature does not exist in an aesthetic vacuum, however, and you should try to find out as much as possible about the context of its production and reception. It is particularly important to read other works by the same author and writings by contemporaries. At this early stage, you may want to restrict your secondary reading to those standard reference works, such as biographies, which are widely available in public libraries. In the long run, however, it pays to read as wide a range of critical studies as possible.

Some students, and tutors, worry that such studies may stifle the development of any truly personal response. But this won't happen if you are alert to the danger and read critically. After all, you wouldn't passively accept what a stranger told you in conversation. The fact that a critic's views are in print does not necessarily make them any more authoritative (as a glance at the review pages of the *TLS* and *London Review of Books* will reveal). So question the views you find: 'Does this critic's interpretation agree with mine and where do we part company?' 'Can it be right to try and restrict this text's meanings to those found by its author or first audience?' 'Doesn't this passage treat a theatrical text as though it were a novel?' Often it is views which you reject which prove most valuable since they challenge you to articulate your own position with greater clarity. Be sure to keep careful notes on what the critic wrote, and your *reactions* to what the critic wrote.

Analyse the question

You cannot begin to answer a question until you understand what task it is you have been asked to perform. Recast the question in your own words and reconstruct the line of reasoning which lies behind it. Where there is a choice of topics, try to choose the one for which you are best prepared. It would, for example, be unwise to tackle 'How far do you agree that in *Paradise Lost* Milton transformed the epic models he inherited from ancient Greece and Rome?' without a working knowledge of Homer and Virgil (or *Paradise Lost* for that matter!). If you do not already know the works of these authors, the question should spur you on to read more widely — or discourage you from attempting it at all. The scope of an essay, however, is not always so obvious and you must remain alert to the implied demands of each question. How could you possibly 'Consider the view that *Wuthering Heights* transcends the conventions of the Gothic novel' without reference to at least some of those works which, the question suggests, have *not* transcended Gothic conventions?

When you have decided on a topic, analyse the terms of the question itself. Sometimes these self-evidently require careful definition: *tragedy* and *irony*, for example, are notoriously difficult concepts to pin down and you will probably need to consult a good dictionary of literary terms. Don't ignore, however, those seemingly innocuous phrases which often smuggle in significant assumptions. 'Does Macbeth lack the nobility of the true tragic hero?' obviously invites you to discuss nobility and the nature of the tragic hero. But what of 'lack' and 'true' — do they suggest that the play would be improved had Shakespeare depicted Macbeth in a different manner? or that tragedy is superior to other forms of drama? Remember that you are not expected meekly to agree with the assumptions implicit in the question. Some questions are deliberately provocative in order to stimulate an engaged response. Don't be afraid to take up the challenge.

Sketch out your preliminary ideas

'Which comes first, the evidence or the answer?' is one of those chicken and egg questions. How can you form a view without inspecting the evidence? But how can you know which evidence is relevant without some idea of what it is you are looking for? In practice the mind reviews evidence and formulates preliminary theories or hypotheses at one and the same time, although for the sake of clarity we have separated out the processes. Remember that these early ideas are only there to get you started. You *expect* to modify them in the light of the evidence you uncover. Your initial hypothesis may be an instinctive 'gut-reaction'. Or you may find that you prefer to 'sleep on the problem', allowing ideas to gell over a period of time. Don't worry in either case. The mind is quite capable of processing a vast amount of accumulated evidence, the product of previous reading and thought, and reaching sophisticated intuitive judgements. Eventually, however, you are going to have to think carefully through any ideas you arrive at by such intuitive processes. Are they logical? Do they take account of all the relevant factors? Do they fully answer the question set? Are there any obvious reasons to qualify or abandon them?

Assemble your evidence

Now is the time to return to the text and re-read it with the question and your working hypothesis firmly in mind. Many of the notes you have already made are likely to be useful, but assess the precise relevance of this material and make notes on any new evidence you discover. The important thing is to cast your net widely and take into account points which tend to undermine your case as well as those that support it. As always, ensure that your notes are full, accurate, and reflect your own critical judgements.

You may well need to go outside the text if you are to do full justice to the question. If you think that the 'Oedipus complex' may be relevant to an answer on *Hamlet* then read Freud and a balanced selection of those critics who have discussed the appropriateness of applying psychoanalytical theories to the interpretation of literature. Their views can most easily be tracked down by consulting the annotated bibliographies held by most major libraries (and don't be afraid to ask a librarian for help in finding and using these). Remember that you go to works of criticism not only to obtain information but to stimulate you into clarifying your own position. And that since life is short and many critical studies are long, judicious use of a book's index and/or contents list is not to be scorned. You can save yourself a great deal of future labour if you carefully record full bibliographic details at this stage.

Once you have collected the evidence, organise it coherently. Sort the detailed points into related groups and identify the quotations which support these. You must also assess the relative importance of each point, for in an essay of limited length it is essential to establish a firm set of priorities, exploring some ideas in depth while discarding or subordinating others.

Test your ideas

As we stressed earlier, a hypothesis is only a proposal, and one that you fully expect to modify. Review it with the evidence before you. Do you really still believe in it? It would be surprising if you did not want to modify it in some way. If you cannot see any problems, others may. Try discussing your ideas with friends and relatives. Raise them in class discussions. Your tutor is certain to welcome your initiative. The critical process is essentially collaborative and there is absolutely no reason why you should not listen to and benefit from the views of others. Similarly, you should feel free to test your ideas against the theories put forward in academic journals and books. But do not just borrow what you find. Critically analyse the views on offer and, where appropriate, integrate them into your own pattern of thought. You must, of course, give full acknowledgement to the sources of such views.

Do not despair if you find you have to abandon or modify significantly your initial position. The fact that you are prepared to do so is a mark of intellectual integrity. Dogmatism is never an academic virtue and many of the best essays explore the *process* of scholarly enquiry rather than simply record its results.

Plan your argument

Once you have more or less decided on your attitude to the question (for an answer is never really 'finalised') you have to present your case in the most persuasive manner. In order to do this you must avoid meandering from point to point and instead produce an organised argument — a structured flow of ideas and supporting evidence, leading logically to a conclusion which fully answers the question. Never begin to write until you have produced an outline of your argument.

You may find it easiest to begin by sketching out its main stage as a flow chart or some other form of visual presentation. But eventually you should produce a list of paragraph topics. The paragraph is the conventional written demarcation for a unit of thought and you can outline an argument quite simply by briefly summarising the substance of each paragraph and then checking that these points (you may remember your English teacher referring to them as topic sentences) really do follow a coherent order. Later you will be able to elaborate on each topic, illustrating and qualifying it as you go along. But you will find this far easier to do if you possess from the outset a clear map of where you are heading.

All questions require some form of an argument. Even so-called 'descriptive' questions *imply* the need for an argument. An adequate answer to the request to 'Outline the role of Iago in *Othello*' would do far more than simply list his appearances on stage. It would at the very least attempt to provide some *explanation* for his actions — is he, for example, a representative stage 'Machiavel'? an example of pure evil, 'motiveless malignity'? or a realistic study of a tormented personality reacting to identifiable social and psychological pressures?

Your conclusion ought to address the terms of the question. It may seem obvious, but 'how far do you agree', 'evaluate', 'consider', 'discuss', etc, are *not* interchangeable formulas and your conclusion must take account of the precise wording of the question. If asked 'How far do you agree?', the concluding paragraph of your essay really should state whether you are in complete agreement, total disagreement, or, more likely, partial agreement. Each preceding paragraph should have a clear justification for its existence and help to clarify the reasoning which underlies your conclusion. If you find that a paragraph serves no good purpose (perhaps merely summarising the plot), do not hesitate to discard it.

The arrangement of the paragraphs, the overall strategy of the argument, can vary. One possible pattern is dialectical: present the arguments in favour of one point of view (**thesis**); then turn to counter-arguments or to a rival interpretation (**antithesis**); finally evaluate the competing claims and arrive at your own conclusion (**synthesis**). You may, on the other hand, feel so convinced of the merits of one particular case that you wish to devote your entire essay to arguing that viewpoint persuasively (although it is always desirable to indicate, however briefly, that you are aware of alternative, if flawed, positions). As the essays contained in this volume demonstrate, there are many other possible strategies. Try to adopt the one which will most comfortably accommodate the demands of the question and allow you to express your thoughts with the greatest possible clarity.

Be careful, however, not to apply abstract formulas in a mechanical manner. It is true that you should be careful to define your terms. It is *not* true that every essay should begin with 'The dictionary defines *x* as . . .'. In fact, definitions are often best left until an appropriate moment for their introduction arrives. Similarly every essay should have a beginning, middle and end. But it does not follow that in your opening paragraph you should announce an intention to write an essay, or that in your concluding paragraph you need to signal an imminent desire to put down your pen. The old adages are often useful reminders of what constitutes good practice, but they must be interpreted intelligently.

Write out the essay

Once you have developed a coherent argument you should aim to communicate it in the most effective manner possible. Make certain you clearly identify yourself, and the question you are answering. Ideally, type your answer, or at least ensure your handwriting is legible and that you leave sufficient space for your tutor's comments. Careless presentation merely distracts from the force of your argument. Errors of grammar, syntax and spelling are far more serious. At best they are an irritating blemish, particularly in the work of a student who should be sensitive to the nuances of language. At worst, they seriously confuse the sense of your argument. If you are aware that you have stylistic problems of this kind, ask your tutor for advice at the earliest opportunity. Everyone, however, is liable to commit the occasional howler. The only remedy is to give yourself plenty of time in which to proof-read your manuscript (often reading it aloud is helpful) before submitting it.

Language, however, is not only an instrument of communication; it is also an instrument of thought. If you want to think clearly and precisely you should strive for a clear, precise prose style. Keep your sentences short and direct. Use modern, straightforward English wherever possible. Avoid repetition, clichés and wordiness. Beware of generalisations, simplifications, and overstatements. Orwell analysed the relationship between stylistic vice and muddled thought in his essay 'Politics and the English Language' (1946) — it remains essential reading (and is still readily available in volume 4 of the Penguin *Collected Essays, Journalism and Letters*). Generalisations, for example, are always dangerous. They are rarely true and tend to suppress the individuality of the texts in question. A remark such as 'Keats always employs sensuous language in his poetry' is not only fatuous (what, after all, does it mean? is *every* word he wrote equally 'sensuous'?) but tends to obscure interesting distinctions which could otherwise be made between, say, the descriptions in the 'Ode on a Grecian Urn' and those in 'To Autumn'.

The intelligent use of quotations can help you make your points with greater clarity. Don't sprinkle them throughout your essay without good reason. There is no need, for example, to use them to support uncontentious statements of fact. 'Macbeth murdered Duncan' does not require textual evidence (unless you wish to dispute Thurber's brilliant parody, 'The Great Macbeth Murder Mystery', which reveals Lady Macbeth's father as the culprit!). Quotations should be included, however, when they are necessary to support your case. The proposition that Macbeth's imaginative powers wither after he has killed his king would certainly require extensive quotation: you would almost certainly want to analyse key passages from both before and after the murder (perhaps his first and last soliloquies?). The key word here is 'analyse'. Quotations cannot make your points on their own. It is up to you to demonstrate their relevance and clearly explain to your readers *why* you want them to focus on the passage you have selected.

Most of the academic conventions which govern the presentation of essays are set out briefly in the style sheet below. The question of gender, however, requires fuller discussion. More than half the population of the world is female. Yet many writers still refer to an undifferentiated *man*kind. Or write of the author and *his* public. We do not think that this convention has much to recommend it. At the very least, it runs the risk of introducing unintended sexist attitudes, and at times leads to such patent absurdities as 'Cleopatra's final speech asserts *man*'s true nobility'. With a little thought, you can normally find ways of expressing yourself which do not suggest that the typical author, critic or reader is male. Often you can simply use plural forms, which is probably a more elegant solution than relying on such awkward formulations as 's/he' or 'he and she'. You should also try to avoid distinguishing between male and female authors on the basis of forenames. Why *Jane* Austen and not *George* Byron? Refer to all authors by their last names unless there is some good reason not to. Where there may otherwise be confusion, say between T S and George Eliot, give the name in full when if first occurs and thereafter use the last name only.

Finally, keep your audience firmly in mind. Tutors and examiners are interested in understanding your conclusions and the processes by which you arrived at them. They are not interested in reading a potted version of a book they already know. **So don't pad out your work with plot summary.**

Hints for examinations

In an examination you should go through exactly the same processes as you would for the preparation of a term essay. The only difference lies in the fact that some of the stages will have had to take place before you enter the examination room. This should not bother you unduly. Examiners are bound to avoid the merely eccentric when they come to formulate papers and if you have read widely and thought deeply about the central issues raised by your set texts you can be confident you will have sufficient material to answer the majority of questions sensibly.

The fact that examinations impose strict time limits makes it *more*, rather than less, important that you plan carefully. There really is no point in floundering into an answer without any idea of where you are going, particularly when there will not be time to recover from the initial error.

Before you begin to answer any question at all, study the entire paper with care. Check that you understand the rubric and know how many questions you have to answer and whether any are compulsory. It may be comforting to spot a title you feel confident of answering well, but don't rush to tackle it: read *all* the questions before deciding which *combination* will allow you to display your abilities to the fullest advantage. Once you have made your choice, analyse each question, sketch out your ideas, assemble the evidence, review your initial hypothesis, plan your argument, *before* trying to write out an answer. And make notes at each stage: not only will these help you arrive at a sensible conclusion, but examiners are impressed by evidence of careful thought.

Plan your time as well as your answers. If you have practised writing timed essays as part of your revision, you should not find this too difficult. There can be a temptation to allocate extra time to the questions you know you can answer well; but this is always a short-sighted policy. You will find yourself left to face a question which would in any event have given you difficulty without even the time to give it serious thought. It is, moreover, easier to gain marks at the lower end of the scale than at the upper, and you will never compensate for one poor answer by further polishing two satisfactory answers. Try to leave some time at the end of the examination to re-read your answers and correct any obvious errors. If the worst comes to the worst and you run short of time, don't just keep writing until you are forced to break off in mid-paragraph. It is far better to provide for the examiner a set of notes which indicate the overall direction of your argument.

Good luck — but if you prepare for the examination conscientiously and tackle the paper in a methodical manner, you won't need it!

short prose quotation incorporated in the text of the essay, within quotation marks.

deceiving Benedick and Beatrice into 'a mountain of affection th'one with th'other' (II.1.339–340). The basis of both plots is getting the victims to overhear other people speaking, as they think, honestly.

In fact, therefore, we are being presented with two types of deceit: that which is benevolent, like Don Pedro's or the Friar's, seeking ultimately a harmony that can be expressed [in] marriage, and that which is totally destructive, like Don [John]. The success of each type of deceit depends on a manipul[ation of] language and an alteration of behaviour and appearances, [and] on the readiness of the victims to judge from what is pre[sented to] their eyes and ears. Telling the two types apart may [be diffic]ult.

[I]t is not as if any character is unaware of the difficult [relat]ionship of appearance to reality: but nearly every one is led [to] [c]hoose, of two alternatives, the wrong one. The best instance [o]f this comes at the crisis of the play:

long verse quotation indented and introduced by a colon. No quotation marks are needed.

Three dots (ellipsis) indicate where words or phrases have been cut from quotation or where (as here) a quotation begins mid-sentence.

> HERO   ... seemed I ever otherwise to you?
> CLAUDIO   Out of thee! Seeming! I will write against it.
>   You seem to me as Dian in her orb,
>   As chaste as is the bud ere it be blown;
>   But you are more intemperate in your blood
>   Than Venus, or those pampered animals
>   That rage in savage sensuality.
>
>   (IV.1.53–59)

Line reference given directly after the quotation, in brackets.

Hero's innocent use of the word 'seemed' — not 'was' — gets Claudio on the raw, for it raises the issue of behaviour versus real nature that is the cause of his torment. It triggers [a] remarkable anticipation of Othello's tortured animal ima[gery] that highlights the emotional perception of the disju[nction] between appearance and what Claudio at this point beli[eves to] be reality. He could not be more wrong; and he is wrong [because] he trusted the suspect word of Don John and what he w[anted] to see at Hero's window rather than the woman he chose to [have] as his wife. Love must, as both Desdemona (*Othello*) and Cordelia (*King Lear*) know, depend on trust: it (or its lack) can never be *proved*. Claudio is given 'ocular proof' (*Othello* III.3.360) of Hero's apparent unchastity, just as Othello is of Desdemona's by Iago, a stage-managing and manipulating

book/play titles are given in italics. In a handwritten or typed manuscript this would appear as underlining: King Lear; Othello.

Short verse quotation incorporated in the text of the essay within quotation marks. If the quotation ran on into a second line of poetry, this would be indicated by a slash (/).

We have divided the following information into two sections. Part A describes those rules which it is essential to master no matter what kind of essay you are writing (including examination answers). Part B sets out some of the more detailed conventions which govern the documentation of essays.

PART A: LAYOUT

Titles of texts

Titles of published books, plays (of any length), long poems, pamphlets and periodicals (including newspapers and magazines), works of classical literature, and films should be underlined: e.g. David Copperfield (novel), Twelfth Night (play), Paradise Lost (long poem), Critical Quarterly (periodical), Horace's Ars Poetica (Classical work), Apocalypse Now (film).

    Notice how important it is to distinguish between titles and other names. Hamlet is the play; Hamlet the prince. Wuthering Heights is the novel; Wuthering Heights the house. Underlining is the equivalent in handwritten or typed manuscripts of printed italics. So what normally appears in this volume as *Othello* would be written as Othello in your essay.

    Titles of articles, essays, short stories, short poems, songs, chapters of books, speeches, and newspaper articles are enclosed in quotation marks; e.g. 'The Flea' (short poem), 'The Prussian Officer' (short story), 'Middleton's Chess Strategies' (article), 'Thatcher Defects!' (newspaper headline).

    Exceptions: Underlining titles or placing them within quotation marks does not apply to sacred writings (e.g. Bible, Koran, Old Testament, Gospels) or parts of a book (e.g. Preface, Introduction, Appendix).

    It is generally incorrect to place quotation marks around a title of a published book which you have underlined. The exception is 'titles within titles': e.g. 'Vanity Fair': A Critical Study (title of a book about *Vanity Fair*).

Quotations

Short verse quotations of a single line or part of a line should be incorporated within quotation marks as part of the running text of your essay. Quotations of two or three lines of verse are treated in the same way, with line endings indicated by a slash(/). For example:

1 In Julius Caesar, Antony says of Brutus, 'This was the noblest Roman of them all'.

2 The opening of Antony's famous funeral oration, 'Friends, Romans, Countrymen, lend me your ears;/ I come to bury Caesar not to praise him', is a carefully controlled piece of rhetoric.

Longer verse quotations of more than three lines should be indented from the main body of the text and introduced in most cases with a colon. Do not enclose indented quotations within quotation marks. For example:

It is worth pausing to consider the reasons Brutus gives to justify his decision to assassinate Caesar:

> It must be by his death; and for my part,
> I know no personal cause to spurn at him,
> But for the general. He would be crowned.
> How might that change his nature, there's the question.

At first glance his rationale may appear logical . . .

Prose quotations of less than three lines should be incorporated in the text of the essay, within quotation marks. Longer prose quotations should be indented and the quotation marks omitted. For example:

1 Before his downfall, Caesar rules with an iron hand. His political opponents, the Tribunes Marullus and Flavius, are 'put to silence' for the trivial offence of 'pulling scarfs off Caesar's image'.

2 It is interesting to note the rhetorical structure of Brutus's Forum speech:

> Romans, countrymen, and lovers, hear me for my cause, and be silent that you may hear. Believe me for my honour, and have respect to mine honour that you may believe. Censure me in your wisdom, and awake your senses, that you may the better judge.

Tenses: When you are relating the events that occur within a work of fiction or describing the author's technique, it is the convention to use the present tense. Even though Orwell published *Animal Farm* in 1945, the book *describes* the animals' seizure of Manor Farm. Similarly, Macbeth always *murders* Duncan, despite the passage of time.

PART B: DOCUMENTATION

When quoting from verse of more than twenty lines, provide line references: e.g. In 'Upon Appleton House' Marvell's mower moves 'With whistling scythe and elbow strong' (l.393).

Quotations from plays should be identified by act, scene and line references: e.g. Prospero, in Shakespeare's The Tempest, refers to Caliban as 'A devil, a born devil' (IV.1.188). (i.e. Act 4. Scene 1. Line 188).

Quotations from prose works should provide a chapter reference and, where appropriate, a page reference.

Bibliographies should list full details of all sources consulted. The way in which they are presented varies, but one standard format is as follows:

1 Books and articles are listed in alphabetical order by the author's last name. Initials are placed after the surname.
2 If you are referring to a chapter or article within a larger work, you list it by reference to the author of the article or chapter, not the editor (although the editor is also named in the reference).
3 Give (in parentheses) the place and date of publication, e.g. (London, 1962). These details can be found within the book itself. Here are some examples:

> Brockbank, J.P., 'Shakespeare's Histories, English and Roman', in Ricks, C. (ed.) English Drama to 1710 (Sphere History of Literature in the English Language) (London, 1971).
> Gurr, A., 'Richard III and the Democratic Process', Essays in Criticism 24 (1974), pp. 39–47.
> Spivack, B., Shakespeare and the Allegory of Evil (New York, 1958).

Footnotes: In general, try to avoid using footnotes and build your references into the body of the essay wherever possible. When you do use them give the full bibliographic reference to a work in the first instance and then use a short title: e.g. See K. Smidt, <u>Unconformities in Shakespeare's History Plays</u> (London, 1982), pp. 43–47 becomes Smidt (pp. 43–47) thereafter. Do not use terms such as 'ibid.' or 'op. cit.' unless you are absolutely sure of their meaning.

There is a principle behind all this seeming pedantry. The reader ought to be able to find and check your references and quotations as quickly and easily as possible. Give additional information, such as canto or volume number whenever you think it will assist your reader.

SUGGESTIONS FOR FURTHER READING

General Studies (containing substantial discussions of *A Midsummer Night's Dream*)

Barber, C L, *Shakespeare's Festive Comedy* (1959)

Bradbury, Malcolm, and Palmer, D J (eds), *Shakespearian Comedy* (1972)

Frye, Northrop, *A Natural Perspective: The Development of Shakespearean Comedy and Romance* (1965)

Kott, Jan, *Shakespeare Our Contemporary*, 2nd edition (1965)

Leggatt, Alexander, *Shakespeare's Comedy of Love* (1973)

Salingar, Alexander, *Shakespeare and the Traditions of Comedy* (1976)

Studies of *A Midsummer Night's Dream*

Calderwood, J L, 'A Midsummer Night's Dream: The Illusion of Drama', *Modern Language Quarterly* 26 (1965), 506–522

Hutton, Virgil, 'A Midsummer Night's Dream: Tragedy in Comic Disguise', *Studies in English Literature* 25 (1985), 289–305

Montrose, Louis Adrian, 'A Midsummer Night's Dream and the Shaping Fantasies of Elizabethan Culture: Gender, Power, Form', in Ferguson, M W, Quilligan, M, and Vickers, N J (eds), *Rewriting the Renaissance: The Discourses of Sexual Difference in Early Modern Europe* (1986), pp. 65–87

Olson, Elder, 'A Midsummer Night's Dream and the Meaning of Court Marriage', *English Literary History* 24 (1957), 95–119

Young, David P, *Something of Great Constancy: The Art of 'A Midsummer Night's Dream'* (1966)

First published 1991
ISBN 0 582 07580 7

*Set in 10/12 pt Century Schoolbook, Linotron 202
Produced through Longman Malaysia , GPS*

Acknowledgement
The editors would like to thank Zachary Leader for his assistance with
the style sheet.